When Churches in Communion Disagree

OTHER TITLES FROM
LIVING CHURCH BOOKS

❆ ❆ ❆

Vol. 1: *God Wills Fellowship*, edited by
Christopher Wells and Jeremy Worthen

When Churches in Communion Disagree

EDITED BY ROBERT HEANEY,
CHRISTOPHER WELLS & PIERRE WHALON

LIVING CHURCH BOOKS

Dallas

iv

Contents

Acknowledgments vii

Contributors. ix

Introduction: Contestation and the Call to Council. 1
Christopher Wells & Pierre Whalon

I   The Grammar of Communion 25
        Katherine Sonderegger

II   Doctrinal Guidelines and Degrees of Communion 37
        George R. Sumner

III   Communion & Disagreement in Acts 15. 51
        Wesley Hill

IV   Mapping Communion and
        Disagreement Ecclesiologically 69
        Jeremy Worthen

V   Ecclesiology and Conflict. 101
        Margaret R. Rose

VI   Seeds of Reconciliation in Kenya 121
        Joseph Wandera

VII   Charles Henry Brent's Way of Unity. 137
        R. William Franklin

VIII   Architecture of Authority. 161
        John Bauerschmidt

vi

ACKNOWLEDGMENTS

The editors of this volume wish to thank Dean Ian Markham and the staff at Virginia Theological Seminary for so kindly welcoming us on January 13-14, 2020, for a consultation on the topic "When Churches in Communion Disagree." We conceived our meeting as a small-scale research conference, sponsored by the House of Bishops Ecclesiology Committee of the Episcopal Church, VTS's Center for Anglican Communion Studies, and the Living Church Foundation. Our goal was simply to present papers and engage in thoughtful conversation about Christian unity within the Episcopal Church, the Anglican Communion, and ecumenically. The travel of several of our scholars was made possible by generous support from the Episcopal dioceses of Texas and Dallas and by Virginia Theological Seminary. Hartley Wensing, Associate Director of the Center for Anglican Communion Studies, organized and managed every detail and provided steady encouragement and kindness the while.

viii

CONTRIBUTORS

❋ The Rt. Rev. Dr. John C. Bauerschmidt is Bishop of Tennessee.

❋ The Rt. Rev. Dr. R. William Franklin was XI Bishop of the Episcopal Diocese of Western New York from 2011 to 2019 and now serves as assisting bishop of the Episcopal Diocese of Long Island.

❋ Dr. Robert S. Heaney is professor of theology and mission at Virginia Theological Seminary.

❋ The Rev. Dr. Wesley Hill serves as associate professor of New Testament at Western Theological Seminary and visiting scholar at Church of the Incarnation, Dallas.

❋ The Rev. Margaret R. Rose serves as Deputy for Ecumenical and Interreligious Relations in the Episcopal Church.

❋ The Rev. Dr. Katherine Sonderegger is William Meade Chair of Systematic Theology at Virginia Theological Seminary.

❋ The Rt. Rev. Dr. George R. Sumner is Bishop of the Diocese of Dallas.

❋ The Rt. Rev. Dr. Joseph Wandera is Bishop of the Diocese of Mumias.

❋ Dr. Christopher Wells is executive director of the Living Church Foundation, based in Dallas.

❋ The Rt. Rev. Pierre Whalon served as the first elected bishop in charge of the Convocation of Episcopal Churches in Europe from 2001 to 2019.

❋ The Rev. Canon Dr. Jeremy Worthen serves as team rector of Ashford Town Parish in the Diocese of Canterbury.

INTRO

Introduction: Contestation and the Call to Council

Christopher Wells & Pierre Whalon

Watch your life and doctrine closely. Persevere in them, because if you do, you will save both yourself and your hearers.

—1 TIM. 4:16

SCHOOLS OF ANGLICAN SYNODALITY

The present collection of essays takes as read and seeks to build upon the 2018 report of the Ecclesiology Committee of the Episcopal Church, "Re-membering and Re-imagining."[1] That report consisted of a collection of articles and a primer by the committee that offered a narrative about the origins of the ecclesiology of the Episcopal Church, set within a broader Anglican and ecumenical ambit. The report showed that the Episcopal Church has been "conciliar" according to a recognizable pattern of self-government and decision-making by synod, with an at least aspirational interest in larger councils and synods of the Church Catholic, starting with the Anglican Communion. In the 19th and 20th centuries, individual Episcopalians especially helped shape wider currents of both Anglican ecclesiology and ecumenical thinking, and often led one and another nascent institution. The question of integral relation between Anglican synods has, however, never been settled, partly because its perennial broaching yields various responses, each of which inspires distinct lines of argument, research, and would-be reform. Anglican ecclesiology has, since at least 1867, the date of the first Lambeth Conference, found itself in a near-constant state of creative, ecumenically influential flux.[2] "Among

---

1 Published in *Sewanee Theological Review*, 61/2 (2018), available online at https://episcopalchurch.org/files/documents/str_ecclesiology_report_2018.pdf.

2 This is the thesis of the essays collected in *The Oxford History of Anglicanism, vol. IV: Global Western Anglicanism, c. 1910–Present*, ed. Jeremy Morris (Oxford: Oxford University Press, 2017). Cf. the review by Christopher Wells, *Religious Studies Review*, 45/2 (2019): 127-28.

those [churches of the Reformation] in which Catholic traditions and institutions in part continue to exist, the Anglican Communion occupies a special place."[3]

The Lambeth Conference has, in fact, since its founding, served as the principal school in Anglican ecclesiological development, even amid—and because of the —near-constant change in social and institutional centers and networks of relation that give flesh to our global family. We write now on the eve of Lambeth Conference 2022, delayed due to both the COVID-19 pandemic and the difficulty of persuading all the bishops of the Communion to attend, just as several provinces, numerically amounting to one third of the members of the Communion, boycotted the last conference of 2008.[4] That the "Lambeth School," to propose a metaphor, has managed to keep its doors open is a marvel, attributable to the celebrated instructors and dogged student body, all of whom have braved a continuously evolving curriculum, shifting standards of evaluation, and on-again-off-again accreditation. Viewed positively, we have specialized in learning by doing, adjusting to new realities in a spirit of openness and trust in God. Rather more experimental in its pedagogical philosophy than many parents have wished (and, truth be told, lurching from one module to another, led now by this reserved institutionalist, that spiritual visionary, and still another restless reformer), the conference has suffered lately from a loss of students to one or two newly chartered ventures that seek to deliver more reliable outcomes, borne

---

3   Second Vatican Council, *Decree on Ecumenism* (1964), §13, available online.

4   For numbers and analysis, see David Goodhew, "Lambeth 2022 and African Anglicanism" on *Covenant* (June 20, 2022), available online.

of objective standards and sustained testing.

Just here, one stubbornly difficult question, among others, facing the churches of the Anglican Communion concerns the reality of autonomous provincial synods arriving at differing conclusions on matters of Christian doctrine. The difficulty of the question presents itself insofar as these churches *seek to be in communion*: seek, that is, when they do not insist that they already are and probably always will be in communion, and/or—on Tuesday, Thursday, and Saturday—admit defeat, allowing that communion is broken, irreparable, and possibly not of particular interest or import anyway. That churches in communion disagree, therefore, the focus of the present volume, not only describes a difficult aspect of our life together at present but also amounts to a question or questions. The fact of disagreement between and among Anglican churches forces us to reckon with what we mean by *disagreement*, a challenge in its own right, and with the meaning of *communion*. Holding the two together scripturally and theologically demands an account of the nature and contours of the Church as given and received, as well-established yet developing, and as constituted in Christ sacramentally, according to the pattern of the Paschal Mystery.

One thinks, in recent Anglican history, of our experience with the ordination of women to the priesthood—first in Hong Kong, Canada, and the Episcopal Church—and subsequently to the episcopate. *The Windsor Report*'s history of this period emphasizes the Communion's ordered process of discernment, reception, and decision-making, centered on successive Lambeth conferences, but the process was not easy, and resulted in reluctant acceptance of "impaired communion," with which we still live today.[5] Our current struggles over marriage and sexuality have, in many ways, reprised and amplified the previous synodical anxiety about ordaining women, underlining again the need to arrive at a common articulation of Anglican structures, sources of doctrine, and decision-making, if and as we can.

To be sure, many believe that we cannot, or perhaps should not try. The differences are too great, the distances between our views and contexts too vast. The Episcopal Church's General Convention of 1976 not only authorized the ordination of women to all three orders but also passed Resolution A069, stating that "homosexual persons are children of God who have a full and equal claim with all other persons upon the love, acceptance, and pastoral concern and care of the Church."[6] Since then, numerous contested questions (not only for Anglicans) have arisen in this field—concerning the proper rights and responsibilities of gay and lesbian Christians, the nature and extent of pastoral care owed to them, appropriate expectations for ordained leaders, especially bishops, and, of course, questions about the teaching of Scripture, received and evolving traditions, wider ecumenical discernments, and a range of canon-legal considerations.

---

5   Lambeth Commission on Communion, *The Windsor Report 2004* (London: Anglican Communion Office & Anglican Consultative Council, 2004), esp. §§12-21 for the history of the Communion's discernment and decision-making about the ordination of women to the priesthood and episcopate. Cf. the well-resourced and far-reaching paper by the General Synod of the Church of England, *Communion and Disagreement: A Report from the Faith and Order Commission* (2016); available online.

6   Episcopal Church, Resolution A069: "Recognize the Equal Claims of Homosexuals" (1976), available online.

Scanning the contemporary Anglican landscape, we see simply at the level of practice a diversity of teaching and discipline on these matters, largely reflective of our varying cultures, though few if any of our churches have reached a comfortable accord or resolution internally. We all struggle with difference and disagreement, as the ground shifts under our feet.

Does the Anglican Communion have a doctrine here? Resolution I.10 of Lambeth Conference 1998 recommended a standard of Communion teaching about homosexuality that has remained a constant touchstone and constant point of conflict, as churches have variously counted upon and sought to move beyond it. Lambeth Conference 2022 will address these questions again, as will the Church of England in its current General Synod, jumping off from the substantive suite of resources gathered as *Living in Love and Faith*. The Episcopal Church accepted a compromise on the matter in Resolution B012 of the 2018 General Convention, which made space for the teaching and practice of self-styled Communion Partner dioceses as a minority voice alongside a majority embrace of same-sex marriage. The 2021 report of the Episcopal Church's Task Force on Communion across Difference, working in the wake of the compromise, suggested that the occasion of its convening might signify a "*kairos* moment, given providentially by God at this time to help Episcopalians and Anglicans find a path forward together."[7]

---

7 Task Force on Communion across Difference, *"Put Out into the Deep Water": Communion across Difference as a Christian Call*, being a Report to the 80th General Convention of the Episcopal Church, 15; available online in *The Blue Book 2021*.

Lofty words but fitting for a would-be "Communion across Difference School," seeking to articulate a theologico-spiritual methodology for persisting patiently in churches and communions characterized by deep disagreement. Structural solutions are not foreclosed in this school, but neither are they forefronted. Rather, something more fundamental and remedial is proposed: a curriculum of compassion, that is, suffering with others, in their company (cf. Matt. 19:14: "suffer the children"), in the hope that God will make clear in time next steps to be taken. Rooted in a clear articulation of baptismal solidarity and a recognition of the mixed-body character of the Church, this School would have us take brothers and sisters at their word when they profess faith in Jesus, even if full communion remains out of reach for now. The "School of Reconciliation" associated with Archbishop Welby and others as an intuitive methodology for muddling along in charity fits here, if we understand it as not foreclosing further structural discernments on principle but simply setting them aside to start.[8]

The Task Force on Communion across Difference sets out its vision in a series of hope-filled rhetorical questions:

---

8   See Justin Welby, *The Power of Reconciliation* (London: Bloomsbury, 2022); Muthuraj Swamy, *Reconciliation: The Archbishop of Canterbury's Lent Book 2019* (London: SPCK, 2018). Cf. *Good Disagreement? Grace and Truth in a Divided Church*, ed. Andrew Atherstone and Andrew Goddard, with a Foreword by the Archbishop of Canterbury (London: Lion Books, 2015); John Bauerschmidt, "Beyond Agreeing to Disagree" (Jan. 13, 2016), available online at livingchurch.org.

Can we view our present disagreements through the lens of a given communion in Christ, and can we imagine ways of walking together that enact the respect, forbearance, and Christian love to which we have long committed ourselves? Stated in terms of the foregoing kinds of communion [namely, baptismal, ecumenical, and denominational]: since we share an initiating and transformative communion in Christ and "have left everything to follow" Jesus (Mt. 19:27), can we express this faithfully despite, and even through, our disagreements over marriage? Can we imagine ways of living together, both affectively and structurally, that will accommodate our difference, and permit us still to say that we share a common faith and order as Episcopalians and as Anglicans—while peering, like our forebears, over the horizon to the larger body of Christ? Finally, if our differences seem quite fundamental, as this Task Force believes they are, might we nonetheless find some old or new means of flexibility ("local adaptation") that could permit us to carry on in one church and one Communion? If so, our witness may again be heard as resounding testimony to the love of Christ in a time of great division in our country, our Communion, and our world.[9]

Presuming a basic commitment to accompanying one another across difference, the task force recognizes that more Faith and Order work remains to be done ("structurally"), and adverts to a need for episcopal leadership in a "locally-adapted" key of creative flexibility. The

9 Task Force on Communion across Difference, *"Put Out into the Deep Water,"* 6.

reference to local adaptation is drawn from the Lambeth Quadrilateral of 1888, marking a reception by the Lambeth Conference of a resolution passed by the House of Bishops of the Episcopal Church at the General Convention meeting in Chicago two years' prior. As the task force report narrates: "Arising from an American context of inter-denominational self-awareness and a pragmatism placed in service of the gospel, Episcopalians seeded the notion that structural differences might be accommodated both between and among Christian denominations." Were this to be retrieved today by Episcopalians and Anglicans as a resource for our struggle to sustain communion-in-disagreement, we might mark this era "as a time when we began giving the gift of the Chicago Quadrilateral to ourselves to enable all to flourish." How so? The task force continues:

> Locally adapted disagreement with respect to marriage might take various forms, ranging from simply deciding to accept [inter-diocesan] diversity, as we have done recently in the Episcopal Church, to more ambitious structural reforms, of a sort that others in the Anglican Communion are attempting. There may be good reasons for both at different times, and some degree of flexibility can aid experimentation on the way to wise and peaceable settlements.[10]

---

10   All from *ibid.*, 5 and 15. Later in the report, the task force calls for more work on "the exercise, role, and range of episcopal ministry, since the ministry of bishops necessarily incorporates local, regional, and worldwide aspects. In a world that seeks to overcome disagreement through enforced uniformities, differentiated communion in an episcopal key may contribute a much-needed leaven of principled diversity, set within provisional structures that model humility" (17).

In these texts, the Task Force on Communion across Difference helpfully adverts to one more school of Anglican ecclesiology, the "Structural School," which seeks to gather, study, and receive proposals for articulating and developing Faith and Order, not only for Anglicans but for all Christians and churches. Traditionally, churches have matriculated into this school in order to think through the properly bounded nature of the Church as an institution (see Augustine of Hippo in the 4th and 5th centuries), and to articulate how a newly defined church should situate itself relative to others in a presumptive Whole (as Richard Hooker did in the 16th century). Since the dawn of the ecumenical era, the Structural School has modified its curriculum to accommodate churches seeking paths to fuller unity with other Christians and, conversely, those seeking paths to amicable differentiation in a baptismal key, explicable with reference to *degrees of communion*.[11]

From Lambeth Conference 1867, to the founding of the Anglican Consultative Council (1968) and Primates' Meeting (1979), to the advent of the Inter-Anglican Theological and Doctrinal Commission (1994), specifically Anglican questions about doctrine, authority, and decision-making have understandably landed in the Structural School—and have taken on an ecumenical hue, by dint of the logic of ecclesiology, rooted as it is in Scripture, sacraments, and early Church precedents. We have mentioned the Chicago-Lambeth

---

11 The latter line of thought renders outdated the old-fashioned notion of *schism*, according to which a clear "separation" was presumed to have taken place, amounting to a break in communion altogether. See *Decree on Ecumenism*, §3.

Quadrilateral as the founding text for Anglican-structural thinking in the Communion era, which rightly should be read with reference to the impassioned prologue published by the Episcopal House of Bishops, enunciating the synodical mandate with an eye to mission: "this church does not seek to absorb other Communions, but rather, co-operating with them on the basis of a common Faith and Order, to discountenance schism, to heal the wounds of the Body of Christ, and to promote the charity which is the chief of Christian graces and the visible manifestation of Christ to the world."[12]

Lambeth Conference 1920's "Appeal to all Christian People" comes next in terms of influence, and still resounds in its clarion call to council:

> We believe that God wills fellowship. By God's own act this fellowship was made in and through Jesus Christ, and its life is in his Spirit. We believe that it is God's purpose to manifest this fellowship, so far as this world is concerned, in an outward, visible, and united society, holding one faith, having its own recognized officers, using God-given means of grace, and inspiring all its members to the world-wide service of the Kingdom of God. This is what we mean by the Catholic Church.[13]

12 Chicago Quadrilateral, 1886 (BCP 1979, 877), available online: http://an-glicansonline.org/basics/Chicago_Lambeth.html. See the helpful discussion of the Quadrilateral by John F. Woolverton, "The Chicago-Lambeth Quadrilateral and the Lambeth Conferences" in *Historical Magazine of the Protestant Episcopal Church*, 53/2 (1984): 95-109, available online.

13 Lambeth Conference 1920, Resolution 9: "Reunion of Christendom." See *God Wills Fellowship: Lambeth Conference 1920 and the Ecumenical*

The Toronto Anglican Congress and its summons to *Mutual Responsibility and Interdependence in the Body of Christ* (1963), the *Virginia* (1997) and *Windsor* (2004) reports, the Anglican Covenant (2009), and 2012's *Towards a Symphony of Instruments*, published by the Inter-Anglican Standing Commission on Unity, Faith and Order, all wrestled for a blessing from the structural curriculum in a key of query. To these, we may now add the current round of discussion by the Anglican-Roman Catholic International Commission, set out in a first of two texts, *Walking Together on the Way: Learning to be the Church—Local, Regional, Universal* (2018). The dialogue team argues for a recovery of ecumenical synodality, of a sort that would challenge both Catholics and Anglicans to press more surely into consultation, consensus, and a right application of subsidiarity, so that the local and the universal (or worldwide) are properly attuned to one another.

The trajectory of this last seems especially pertinent as the Anglican Communion has turned more and more to ecumenical ecclesiology to explain its own "internal" life. Ours is a collocation of churches with historic connections, called—we are saying, with both hope and trepidation—to walk together as an icon of charity-in-difference, recognizing how difficult that is. Walking together need not mean walking abreast, or even at the same pace. As the primates noted in 2016, it is possible for pilgrims to advance together along the same road of visible discipleship and obedience at a distance from one another—indeed, even differentiated from one another, out of respect

Vocation of Anglicanism, ed. Christopher Wells and Jeremy Worthen (Dallas: Living Church Books, 2022).

for varying views and needs.[14] The Anglican Covenant, for all its limitations, recognized this when it offered "intensified" communion for those desiring it, with freedom for churches to "opt-in" (in the words of then-Archbishop Rowan Williams) or otherwise take a pass on grounds of conscience or differently discerned vocation.[15] Something like this may still be the best way forward, and in any case is an option on the table, as in the proposed "Covenantal Structure for the Global South Fellowship of Anglican Churches" (adopted in 2019, updated in 2021), proffered as both complement and supplement to the

---

14 Communiqué and Addendum from the Primates' Meeting, "Walking Together in the Service of God in the World" (Canterbury Cathedral, Jan. 2016); available online. Cf. the paper by John Bauerschmidt et al., "The Way of Anglican Communion: Walking Together before God" (May 2017), published by the Communion Partners; available online at communionpartners.org.

15 The Anglican Communion Covenant, 4.1.1: "Each Church freely offers this commitment to other Churches in order to live more fully into the ecclesial communion and interdependence which is foundational to the Churches of the Anglican Communion"; 4.1.3: "Such mutual commitment does not represent submission to any external ecclesiastical jurisdiction. Nothing in this Covenant of itself shall be deemed to alter any provision of the Constitution and Canons of any Church of the Communion, or to limit its autonomy of governance. The Covenant does not grant to any one Church or any agency of the Communion control or direction over any Church of the Anglican Communion"; 4.1.4: "Every Church of the Anglican Communion, as recognised in accordance with the Constitution of the Anglican Consultative Council, is invited to enter into this Covenant according to its own constitutional procedures." Cf. ibid., 3.1.2; 3.2. Cf. Rowan Williams, "The Challenge and Hope of Being an Anglican Today: A Reflection for the Bishops, Clergy and Faithful of the Anglican Communion" (June 27, 2006), available online.

Anglican Communion as currently organized.[16] As one, prominent course of study in the Structural School, covenantal proposals seeks to recover and reclaim the ideal of visible consensus so memorably vindicated in the Chicago Quadrilateral and at Lambeth 1920.

TAKING COUNSEL IN THE WORD MADE FLESH

If the foregoing captures, in broad strokes, the state of Anglican syn-odality today, then we are well on the way of agreeing about *how*, at least, to pursue a common Faith and Order. All sides of our current disputes agree that teaching matters. All agree that truth is of utmost concern, in the person of Christ and for his disciples. And all pro-fess that God's people, throughout the scriptures, are summoned to obedience and unity, in accord with God's character and law, finally and fully expressed in the gospel with which the Church is entrusted. God is faithful, seeking to reconcile all persons, both Jew and Gentile, within the "commonwealth of Israel," through the body and blood of Christ. "For he is our peace; in his flesh he has made both into one and has broken down the dividing wall, that is, the hostility be-tween us" (Eph 2:12, 14). In the School of the Word Made Flesh, all

16 The text may be found on the website of the Global South Fellowship of Anglican Churches at https://www.thegsfa.org/. For an introduction and analysis, see Mark Michael, "Global South Anglicans Launch New Covenant," available online at livingchurch.org.

Christians can learn to seek, serve, and imitate his counsel, not least in our deliberations and decisions with one another.

To this end, we believe it will be helpful to consider anew what we mean by *doctrine* in the context of Christian ecclesial life. This is the focus of the present volume of essays. More than propositional truth, and different in kind from the experiential-expressivism of late modernity, doctrine in its fullness refers to a way of life, set forth in and for community, with its own Christ-formed grammar.[17] From the earliest Church through the Middle Ages, this was how our forebears thought about the pattern of Christian teaching. "Sacred doctrine," in Thomas Aquinas's term of art, comprehends "all things" through God's wisdom in the Word incarnate, in and through whom the faithful may be drawn into a transformative experience of trinitarian communion. In such a theocentric setting, doctrinal discussions between Christians and churches, including varying estimations of right teaching, can find their orientation in God's speech and action, not least sacramentally, which set the terms for shared life in Christ.[18]

---

17 See George A. Lindbeck, *The Nature of Doctrine: Religion and Theology in a Postliberal Age*, 25th anniversary edn. with new intro. by Bruce D. Marshall and new afterword by author (Louisville: Westminster John Knox, 2009).

18 See Thomas Aquinas, *Summa theologiae* I 1 *et passim*. Channeling Aquinas's theocentrism as the basis for her systematic theology, see now Katherine Sonderegger, *Systematic Theology*, vol. 1: *The Doctrine of God* and vol. 2: *The Doctrine of the Holy Trinity: Processions and Persons* (Minneapolis: Fortress, 2015 and 2020). Cf. Wesley Hill's review, "A Twenty-First Century Anglican Divine" on *Covenant* (Dec. 9, 2021), available online. Borrowing a page from Thomas on analogy, see Rowan Williams, *Christ the Heart of Creation* (London: Bloomsbury Continuum,

Katherine Sonderegger and **George Sumner** explicitly employ this model in their essays here.

For leaders charged with forming and defending the faith of the Church, the needed doctrine or teaching may be derived exegetically and ascetically under the sign of the Word. To speak doctrinally is to set forth, organize, and interact with what is given in Scripture, creed, and sacrament "from the beginning: what we have heard, what we have seen with our eyes, what we have looked at and touched with our hands, concerning the word of life" (1 John 1:1). In the communion of God's speaking and acting in creation and redemption, the faithful are transformed "by the washing of water by the word" (Eph. 5:26), writ large as a figure of all the sacraments. Through the Daily Office and personal devotions, Christians find their sorrows and longings wholly anticipated, situated, and inscribed within God's life, enacted by his Son and the Holy Spirit, in order that many may be reborn and gathered into the "Israel of God" (Gal. 6:16). Within this space, which is the universal Church of Christ's Body throughout all ages, we learn, by the mercy of God, to present our own bodies and minds "as a living sacrifice, holy and acceptable to God, which is [our] reasonable act of worship" (Rom. 12:1).[19]

In this ancient sacrificial pattern, the *doctrina* of Old and New Testaments becomes our prayer, bearing witness to Christ as speaker and subject of all the law and the prophets, psalter, gospels, epistles,

---

2018). Cf. Pierre Whalon's review in *Journal of Anglican Studies*, 17/2 (2019): 235-41.

19   See Augustine of Hippo, *Teaching Christianity* (*De Doctrina Christiana*), trans. Edmund Hill (Hyde Park: New City Press, 1995).

and Apocalypse, comprising a singular Word. By the genius of our lectionaries, built on the conviction that "Christ is the same yesterday, today, and forever" (Heb. 13:8), we see day by day the teaching of patriarchs and apostles amazingly fused with, and fulfilled in, the words and actions of Jesus. "The Lord said to my Lord, 'Sit at my right hand, until I make your enemies your footstool'" (Ps. 110:1; Matt. 22:44). On the arrival of the promised Messiah, fulfilled in our hearing (Luke 4:21), St. John can recapitulate the whole of history in a singular vision of Christ and the Church, united at the marriage supper of the Lamb, where the "true words of God" are spoken by the faithful who hold "the testimony of Jesus" (Rev. 19:9-10).

The first Christians assumed this mantle of Christ-formed speech and centered their doctrinal discernments in councils given to sifting the scriptures to account for the worship of Jesus as God. How to understand and speak about the astonishing fact that God became man? As heresies were ruled out, one by one (Marcionism, Gnosticism, Arianism), the decentralized Church took several centuries to articulate a doctrine of the Incarnation of the Word, properly codified in a "Nicene" form in 381. Further inquiry into the person and natures of Christ yielded tragic division,[20] while a mostly-unified Church

---

20 The resulting "Church of the East" or "Nestorian Church" grew enormously in size and sophistication, with missionary efforts reaching through present-day China to the Pacific Ocean. Today the Chaldean and Assyrian churches of Iraq, its tiny remnant, have achieved rapprochement with the Catholic Church, following the 1994 landmark Common Christological Declaration. For an introduction, see Philip Jenkins, *The Lost History of Christianity: The Thousand-Year Golden Age of the Church in the Middle East, Africa, and Asia-and How It Died* (New York: HarperOne, 2009).

persevered through several more councils, up to 787 A.D., marking a symbolic end of the earliest apostolic period. A great schism between East and West followed in 1054, before the western Church flew into dozens, then hundreds and thousands, of pieces during and after the Reformation period of the 16th century up to the present day, most of which divisions have yet to be healed.

If this last sounds depressingly fissiparous, it is. And yet all Christians confess their faith in the one, holy, catholic, and apostolic Church. This means that scripturally, sacramentally, and by the divinely merciful hand of God, the one Church and her singular faith and baptism perdure providentially across space and time and may *still* be encountered by the faithful followers of Jesus. This also is a great mystery (Eph. 5:32), precisely as an outward sign of an inward and spiritual reality. As sacrament, the Church, formed out of Christ's passion, embodies his crucified word, which he shares in love. "You must sit down, says Love, and taste my meat."[21]

In this spirit of Jesus, who loved his own till the end, and promised Peter that "the gates of Hades will not prevail" (Matt. 16:18), Christians have dared to trust that a certain indefectibility inheres in the Church, as a divine grace.[22] So far from serving as a veiled expression of a will to power, as we sometimes fear is lurking around every corner, this doctrine of the Church's faithful perduring amid sustained unfaithfulness and betrayal by her members amounts to a

---

21   George Herbert, "Love (III)," available online.

22   See Anglican-Roman Catholic International Commission, *Authority in the Church I* §18 (1976) and *Authority in the Church II* §23 (1981), available online.

confession of God's sovereignty. The Church survives always and only by God's mercy. This being so, chastened ecclesiality may simply and gratefully, as **John Bauerschmidt** argues, rest in the most basic constituents of order given by God to the primitive Church: Scripture and the apostolic office. Resisting scientistic temptations to inerrancy and pneumatic demonstrability, scriptural and episcopal counsel travel the pilgrim path of faith seeking understanding, aimed at ready agreement with God and our brothers and sisters (see Matt. 5:23-26).

Just here, the double commandment of love, as a summary of Christian teaching and life, serves as the evangelical lodestar of ecclesiological doctrine: to love God with all one's heart, soul, and mind, and one's neighbor as oneself (Mt. 22:37-40; Mk. 12:30-31). We pull toward one another because God in Christ first drew near to us with an unmerited love, "poured into our hearts through the Holy Spirit" (Rom. 5:5). When we love, we do so as enabled by God's primary and effective love in Christ, who perpetually surrenders himself as "a fragrant offering and sacrifice to God" (Eph. 5:2; cf. 1 John 4:19).

Because our Lord Jesus was born, died, resurrected, and ascended, and because he left us his Spirit, we, his friends, know that we can take up our own crosses and follow his way of obedient submission in love to the Father. Of course, our proud hearts and proud divisions are difficult to overcome. Here, St. Paul speaks a word for the wayward: "Should we continue in sin in order that grace may increase? By no means! How can we who died to sin go on living in it? Do [we] not know that all of us who were baptized into Christ Jesus were baptized into his death? Therefore we were buried with him by baptism into death, so that, just as Christ was raised from the dead by the glory of the Father, so we also might walk in newness of life" (Rom. 6:1-4). We denominationalist Christians, long accustomed to impaired communion, would do well to pay heed.

But how shall we get started? The Church has always taught that right doctrine, if truly held, begets charity, and vice versa. God's grace makes this possible, cooperating with the assent of faith and the consent to follow where the Lord leads. Each baptized person must be able to say, "I believe" (*credo*). But God quickens our spirits, outfitting us with faith, hope, and love, called *theological virtues* because they are gifts.

Pierre's sister Françoise was one of the finest Christians he has known, despite the fact that she suffered from Down's syndrome. She would not have understood Christian doctrine intellectually. Yet she treated others with a deep, trusting love, irrespective of status or any other distinguishing feature. The very few people whom Françoise did not care for were those we would do well to avoid ourselves! Beyond the circle of family and regular attendance at church, she moved many by the depth and seriousness with which she took love of neighbor.[23] We see here something of what Aquinas identified as the ideal Christian: an "unlettered old woman" (or man) who accepts the faith simply and readily with joy and responds directly in hope and love, enabled by grace.[24]

---

23 Sometimes the preacher would be startled to hear a deep alto voice crying a well-deserved, "Oh come on!" Françoise Marthe Whalon entered Larger Life on December 9, 2014, at the age of 52. Her funeral took place in a packed church.

24 See Bruce D. Marshall, "*Quod Scit una Vetula*: Aquinas on the Nature of Theology" in *The Theology of Thomas Aquinas*, ed. Rik Van Nieuwenhove and Joseph Wawrykow (Notre Dame: University of Notre Dame Press, 2005).

The point bears directly on the Christ-formed call to communion, which has never been easy. Read the New Testament for a sustained study in disagreement and contestation. But the answer is clear: "Show me your faith apart from works, and I by my works will show you faith," writes St. James (Jas. 2:18). If sacred doctrine amounts to a formative practice in discipleship and holiness after the Word made flesh, then obedience must feature prominently in our ecclesiology. Jesus says: "Those who love me will keep my word, and my Father will love them, and we will come to them and make our home with them" (John 14:23). We will find ourselves able to serve the faith and order of the Church as our lives are turned outward in service, that is, in works, as **Margaret Rose** skillfully demonstrates. This is the great insight of grass-roots ecumenism: that patience and courage, properly applied to the things God loves, can only bear fruit, "thirty and sixty and a hundredfold" (Mark 4:20). We must pray the Lord to send out many laborers into this harvest of communion-in-disagreement, expertly mapped by **Jeremy Worthen**: to reap and prune, sow and fertilize, and not to grow weary, year by year (Matt. 9:38; cf. Luke 13:6-9, John 4:38).

This sends us back to the schools of synodality with which we began. The only plausible solution to entrenched disagreement in the Church has always been council: locally, trans-locally, and universally. Hard to pull off, and by turns enervating and invigorating, taking consensus-driven counsel enables unity in mission. When we fail to agree, in-fighting and competition carry the day, and undermine the witness of the gospel. **Joseph Wandera** bears witness to this truth in his summons to synod. As **Wesley Hill** shows, the pattern finds its origin in the Jerusalem Council of Acts 15, charged with addressing a genuine moral and theological disagreement in the apostolic community. The same spirit of synodality enkindled the Faith and Order movement some 1900 years later, as seen in the inspiring story of Charles Henry Brent, told with devotion by **R. William Franklin**.

To "have the mind of Christ" is, St. Paul insists, to put on God's own wisdom in his Spirit, without which we have lost our way (1 Cor. 2:12-16). To cultivate Christ's mind requires, in turn, a commitment to "wait for one another" as part and parcel of "discerning the body," under God's just oversight (1 Cor. 11:33, 29). "When we are judged by the Lord, we are disciplined so that we may not be condemned along with the world" (11:32). But discipline speaks to repentance and conversion, as features of faithful following.[25] Of course, we confess our sin to God in every authorized liturgy of the Church. We must practice doing so with one another, even publicly, starting with our leaders.[26]

---

25   See Bernard Lonergan's account of conversion in *Method in Theology*, eds. Robert M. Doran and John D. Dadosky (Toronto: University of Toronto Press, 2017), 224ff. On the significance of this today, see Karen Petersen Finch, "Lonergan's Method as Scaffolding for Ecumenical Discernment" in *Receptive Ecumenism: Listening, Learning and Loving in the Way of Christ*, ed. Vicky Balabanski and Geraldine Hawkes (Adelaide, S.A.: ATF Press, 2018), 37-48; Jeremy Wilkins, "Why Lonergan Still Matters," available online.

26   We have good examples here, but we need more. Pope John Paul II apologized publicly hundreds of times during his long pontificate. See the rich discussion of the International Theological Commission in its paper, *Memory and Reconciliation: The Church and the Faults of the Past* (1999), available online.

On pain of the coherence of the gospel and the authenticity of the Church as its bearer, there can be no escaping the call to council, which necessarily follows from communion with God. Let us, therefore, not tire in striving to heed the prayer of our Lord that his disciples "may become completely one, so that the world may know" the love of God in his Son Jesus Christ (John 17:23). And let us "consider how to provoke one another to love and good deeds, not neglecting to meet together, as is the habit of some, but encouraging one another, and all the more as you see the Day approaching" (Heb. 10:24-25). Face to face, with humility, in charity, we Anglicans, and all our brothers and sisters in the Body, shall know the truth, and the truth shall set us free.

ONE

The Grammar of Communion

Katherine Sonderegger

There are seasons in the Church's life, as in all things living, and those seasons may be long and admixed with silence. In the Anglican corner of the Body of Christ, *The Windsor Report* of 2004 has enjoyed a brief season of conversation, debate, and testing; but has now entered into that season of silence, a quiet passing over of its insights, recommendations, and urgent warnings.[1] As with any living being under the Lordship of Christ, the Church exemplifies complex reasons for its speech and for its silence; I do not want to neglect or pass over these matters with an impatient hand. But I think it may be time for our

---

1   See the Lambeth Commission on Communion, *The Windsor Report 2004* (London: Anglican Communion Office & Anglican Consultative Council, 2004), available online.

Communion to take up *Windsor* with fresh ears, to listen for a fresh word about the path forward for us all—a path that is not a highway, clear and laid straight.

I wish to commend *The Windsor Report* for its concision, the precision and scope of its theological judgements, and the structures it proposes for our way forward. I especially want to commend it for its plain speaking.

It seems that many of us in the North American branch of the Communion are no longer able to bear straight-forward discussion of homosexuality. We are inclined to act or to believe it is "all behind us," as is often said, or too personal, too intimate, too deeply integrated into the mystery of the human person, to be debated or discussed or regulated. Teaching in a U.S. seminary, I have real sympathy for this position. I have listened to my students wrestle with homosexuality and with the place of partnered gay people in the Church and its offices since I joined the faculty in 2002. For each of them, this is a fresh question, a fresh struggle, a fresh intimacy to be exposed or judged; but not for me! Always there is need for fresh teaching, fresh exegesis, fresh ecclesiology in the midst of all that seems old, or worn, or painfully neuralgic, including for those of us here locally who lived through the divisions that tore the heart of the Diocese of Virginia.

The truth is that *The Windsor Report* is right—or so it seems to me—that the matter of homosexuality is not closed, not behind us, not settled, and most certainly not forgotten in the Communion to which we belong. The report points out the sharp distinction to be drawn with debates over order, a matter also not settled in the Anglican Communion. The contrast between women's orders, even to the episcopal office, and those of partnered gay people, cannot be easily reduced to single factors. The matter of sexuality will always be more explosive, more intimate, more tactile than will be gender. It can be hidden in ways not readily available to gendered or ethnic human bodies. Indeed, our culture still (though less than many others) treasures a *reserve* and restraint about sexual matters, and the tangled depths of our sexual desires is a history we hope can remain private. Sexuality will transgress borders and it will shock. Freud's warm recommendation of sublimation is testimony to the volcanic power of the sexual drive, even for one as expert in this terrain as was Freud.[2] There are elements that emerge out of contemporary U.S. culture, itself a fractured and decidedly unintegrated polity when it comes to practices, norms, and ideals of human sexuality, including homosexuality. To marry all of this with religious piety is perhaps a more explosive mixture than any of us envisioned.

But *The Windsor Report* considers one critical element in the case of ordaining women to the priesthood: consultation across the Communion. The report holds that the Province of Hong Kong and the North American churches consulted the Archbishop of Canterbury and the primates in several ways and over several decades. The very great patience shown by the innovating provinces—and by the women whose vocation was under debate—is extraordinary and should be laid to heart. Generations of women greeted that promise from afar but did not enter into it. I who have been given this unshadowed honor of ordination can only be grateful for such long

---

2 Freud made use of this notion from his earliest writings, but might be especially pertinent in his late work, *Civilization and its Discontents*, trans. J. Strachey (New York: W. W. Norton Publishing, 1961).

faithfulness and stubborn courage.

I think something like this grace-filled and demanding patience is required for us now about homosexuality. It is hard for many in the United States to remember how brief this revolution in practice and endorsement has been. In my own lifetime (even at this age, not so very long!) the U.S. culture has moved, not altogether and not without deep resistance, from Stonewall to Marriage Equality. This is a heartbeat in the struggle for emancipatory causes, a mere moment in the long march toward race equality or the dignity of native peoples. The debate about homosexuality—its probity; its health or injury; its relation to Holy Scripture; its inwardness and embodied characteristics; its place as exemplar or as warning: all these have had only the beginnings of theological reflection, were we to measure by the generations-long record of feminist and abolitionist argument.

It may seem to many in my church, the Episcopal Church, that this scholarly and ecclesial debate has been nearly everlasting and has consumed several decades of our synodical life. I do not deny the level of textual, historical, and ecclesial research that has been produced in North America—it is important, essential work. I do want to underscore the unfinished work that remains. This scholarship needs to be brought into the heart of the Communion; into face to face, patient work with dissenting groups in the Episcopal Church and beyond; and into inter-religious dialogue. We must reason together. We need to have the whole debate in fresh ways that build on *The Windsor Report*, in an unexpected fashion.

※ ※ ※

We should not forget *Windsor*'s recommendation that the Anglican Communion explore an avenue of more formal unity, either through a common canon law or a Covenant. While the latter option was pursued, it did not prove workable, at least for the time being. Archbishop Welby has made clear that he is not attracted to this solution, but *The Windsor Report* holds several other proposals, perhaps in quiet reserve, that may be fruitful in the midst of division. Folded into the careful discussion of "Section B: Fundamental Principles" are reflections upon two forms of ecclesial distinction that may serve us well today: subsidiarity and matters *adiaphora*. Each has deep theological and ecclesial grounding: one in the work leading up to the Second Vatican Council and the other in the churches of the magisterial Reformation.[3]

I want to focus on the *structural* relation that *The Windsor Report* uncovers between the two. *Windsor* says that subsidiarity and matters *adiaphora* are *paired*, such that the closer the decision is to the local church, the stronger its decisions may be considered matters indifferent to broader networks of communion. The report mentions flowers arrangements on parish altars—not the subject-matter of primatial attention or Lambeth reports. More significantly, *Windsor* refers to the Ceremonies Paragraph of the 1662 prayer book, where local use in liturgical custom and native habit are held to be discretionary to the

---

3 See the Documents of Vatican II, trans. A. Flannery (Grand Rapids: Eerdmans,1984), esp. the Constitution on the Church, *Lumen Gentium*, ch. 4, "On the Laity." For matters *adiaphora*, the classic text is the Formula of Concord, ch. X. This pattern is followed in the famous preface to the Book of Common Prayer (1549), and the articles XXI and XXXIV of the Articles of Religion.

worship and obedience of the Church Catholic. The force of this section, though never fully articulated, suggests that some members of the U.S. and Canadian churches have treated homosexuality as a matter indifferent, and subject to local custom, determination, and culture. The pronounced autonomy of my church and the Canadian church in developing marriage rites or services of blessing for homosexual couples seems to illustrate this natural pairing, assumed but not argued for, between *adiaphora* and local control. We have made this move in our culture, the decisions seemed to say, and we are acting on them.

It would be well worth exploring historically and ecclesiologically whether this analysis holds good. But quite apart from its argumentative soundness, *Windsor* objects strongly to it. The matter of homosexuality, *The Windsor Report* says, is far from indifferent; it has fractured the Communion in ways sharper and more alienating than any of the other debates across the global Church. *Windsor* holds that the place of homosexual persons in the offices of the Church must be brought to the highest levels of communal debate—to doctrinal commissions, primates' gatherings, the archbishop's office, and, of course, to the Lambeth Conference. The notion of provincial autonomy, *Windsor* warns, can be understood ecclesially only as a matter of agency within a larger whole, a distinction and difference that can be held only within a larger unity and coherence.

❊ ❊ ❊

We stand now on the other side of these decisions and *The Windsor Report*. What might we propose as an avenue forward that listens still to this report and its warnings?

I suggest that we consider another distinction that has aided the Roman Catholic Church: the ecclesial idea of a "difference of schools." This distinction differs from matters indifferent in that it touches profound theological matters, central to the entire Church. Yet it implies an abiding difference that does not fracture unity. The "difference of schools" came into its own in the Tridentine era of the Catholic Reformation, beginning with the debate among Spanish theologians over the delicate matter of divine knowledge of future contingent events.[4] This debate embroiled some of Rome's most skilled dialecticians: Bañez the Thomist, Molina the Jesuit, Cardinal Bellarmine, and two sophisticated papal theologians, Clement VIII and Paul V. The debates over middle knowledge, future contingents, effective grace, and omniscience and human freedom stretched over *decades*. Councils were called; pamphlets released in 16th-century style, like bullet fusillades; then Vatican hearings; and finally, oral debates before two popes, in a kind of Supreme Court briefing that ran generations. It has been called the most conceptually sophisticated ecclesial debate in the history of the Church, and, in my view, rivals the delicate christological debates of the post-Cyrillian age, under Justinian and Maximus.

In the aftermath of this debate, no resolution was reached. This is well worth pondering, as it was hardly a theologoumenon—merely

---

4 For these ecclesial and doctrinal debates, see Robert J. Matara, *Divine Causality and Human Free Choice* (Leiden: Brill, 2016); Mirko Skarica, *The Problem of God's Foreknowledge and Human Free Action in Spanish Philosophy* (Washington, D.C.: Catholic University Press, 1997); and the superb introduction to Luis de Molina, *On Divine Foreknowledge* (Ithaca, N.Y.: Cornell University Press, 1988) by Alfred Freddoso.

adiaphora. These theologians debated the very nature of God, the *scopus* and perfection of his knowledge, the workings of his victorious grace, and the freedom of his creatures as they looked into a world filled with duties, with ambiguities and possibilities, and an impenetrable veil drawn across the future. At this level of doctrinal seriousness, no final verdict was reached. The painful calumnies, the calls for inquisition and condemnation, the relentless polemics, personal and ecclesial: these had to stop. But the explosive argument between Thomists and Molinists—or, perhaps better, between two ways of receiving the heritage of the sainted doctor—needed now be regarded as a "difference of the schools." The phrase bespeaks an insoluble difference *in the midst of unity*.

We have had nowhere near the extensive nor sophisticated debate over homosexuality that marked the wars between Thomists and Jesuits. I propose that we have them. I believe there are different schools of argument at work in the Communion as a whole: in exegesis, in Church history, in human anthropology, and in doctrine. We have enunciated these in the modern version of the Reformation pamphlet wars—broadsides designed for supporters to read and cheer—and scholarly articles in journals, especially in North American settings. And, certainly, there have been ecclesial documents, from the *Virginia* and *Windsor* reports to Lambeth statements, *To Set our Hope on Christ* (issued by the Episcopal Church in response to *Windsor*), circular letters, and so forth. But the next step beckons us: to do these kinds of papers, debates, and engagements with members across the Communion, in full view of the Communion, so to speak. We need the conciliar expression of these debates, as the Church has always had in her long history. There are deep, sophisticated, and vital positions to develop on both sides of this issue, and perhaps several more in the interstices. (The current ambiguity about gender in some circles within North American culture tells me that some deeper reflection on sexuality and bodily identity will soon need to come under theological reasoning.[5])

Perhaps in indirect parallel with the *Congregatio de Auxiliis*, these modern school debates may take the life of the human creature, its sexuality in the midst of its obedience and disobedience, and examine it in light of God's knowledge, will, and direction, all in dependence upon Holy Scripture. *To Set our Hope on Christ* took as its parallel or grounding the Spirit poured out on Gentiles in these last days in order to note the gifts of the Spirit discerned in faithful, partnered, monogamous gay Christians. This need not be an argument from experience, which those schooled by Barth (as I have been) may not find compelling. But how it makes use of human history under the providence of God (another central category in Barth's thinking) could well be developed, specified, and grounded.[6] Perhaps the positions developed by the visionary ecumenist Margaret O'Gara[7] could be employed in

5   Two theologians who are beginning to shape our thought in these matters: Mayra Rivera, *The Poetics of the Flesh* (Durham, N.C.: Duke University Press, 2015), and Scott MacDougall, "Bodily Communions: An Eschatological Proposal for Addressing the Christian Body Problem," *Dialog* 57 (2018): 178-85.

6   Consider, for example, the way Barth distinguishes and unites the "greater and lesser lights" in *Church Dogmatics* IV.3, para. 69.2, or the "riddles of world occurrence" in *CD* III.3, para. 49.3.

7   See Margaret O'Gara, *No Turning Back: The Future of Ecumenism*, ed. Michael Vertin (Collegeville, MN: Liturgical Press, 2014).

these doctrinal debates. Are there positions that merit condemnation but have now entered into the past? Can a way forward be forged with new communities, free from the same strictures?

The school position that holds homosexual acts to be incompatible with Holy Scripture—still the unrescinded official view of the Anglican Communion—can be developed also in light of the creaturely gifts, callings, and aims of homosexual persons, and the particular vocation that celibacy and self-discipline has offered to Christians over many centuries. The work of Robert Song comes particularly to mind here. I would not want to pre-judge any of the careful theological positions that might be developed. I do believe that they could be held in respect, with intellectual integrity, and above all with Christian charity. There is far too little of any of these virtues in our current debates *and* in our current silence.

This matter may well mark a difference of schools in the final, obdurate sense. We may never agree. We may be left with baroque Thomists and Molinists who simply cannot countenance each other's primary commitments. But the aim of this entire distinction is to find a way forward: to see a distinction that abides in unity. We are not there yet. We need very great patience to take up this work. But if accord cannot be reached, we may still come to see that in one Church, and one Communion, a difference of schools can be tolerated, even welcomed.

All this unfolds under the great wing of God's merciful guidance, and so I can only confess hope and confidence that God is working his purpose out, even with us, even with me. *The Windsor Report* has given our Anglican Communion many gifts, but perhaps the greatest of them is the call to break our silence and our stubborn hearts, and begin to speak, to write, and to listen.

TWO

Doctrinal Guidelines and Degrees of Communion

George R. Sumner

AUTONOMY IN COMMUNION

It was the folk sage Yogi Berra who famously said, "déjà vu all over again!" Imagine a gathering to think about Anglican ecclesiology, its trinitarian underpinnings, its use of concepts like *reception* and *subsidiarity*, worked out with a view to the instruments of communion. Avail yourselves of the good offices of Virginia Seminary to think about, and beyond, a perceived crisis of Anglican unity.

While that could describe the occasioning conference of this book, I have in mind the deliberations that resulted in *The Virginia*

Report (1997), a quarter of a century ago. Soon thereafter Lambeth 1998 and its resolution I.10 followed, then the Diocese of New Westminster and the election of Gene Robinson, and so on, including the formation of the Anglican Church of North America. The worry that the structures of the Communion would not be equal to these centrifugal forces seems to have been well founded. I want to encourage more theological attention in our church, not less, yet we might wonder what to hope for from another conference or book. We need to be honest and modest in our goals, as befits theological work in service of communion across difference in this "day of little things" (Zech. 4:10).

Let us start with the uncontroversial, if still challenging, aspects of the obstacle course before us. The churches of the Anglican Communion, when they meet in synods and conventions, are autonomous in their self-government. They have the power to make decisions, even if they are troublesome to other provinces. The question is not whether they can, but whether they should. These churches stand in a relation to one another—again not so much in legal ways, but in spiritual and theological ones, which are no less real. We still hope to hearken to the call, originally from the 1963 Anglican Congress in Toronto, to be mutually responsible and interdependent, one with another. We are autonomous, but we are not islands. The Preamble to the Constitution of the Episcopal Church, to take one example, commits us to the historical faith and worship of the apostolic tradition. Between these two realities, autonomy and communion, we struggle to find our way.

Our own Bishop Bill Franklin has written of the need to balance the autonomy of a local religious community within the coherence of a universal church.[1] We must indeed strive to achieve this balance, since there is no clear referee to whom we can repair: no king as in the early period of Anglican history, and no universal primate like the pope. Again, we cannot deny that churches understanding themselves to be bound together in Communion with one another may act in such a way as to lead to strong and continuing disagreement over doctrine. The tension is built into our ecclesiology.

In my earlier essay for the Ecclesiology Committee of our House of Bishops,[2] I spoke of an "ecology" within which doctrinal decisions are made, one in which the wider Communion of Anglican churches forms the background. This is where the principle of conciliarism has a role to play. We may illustrate with reference to the Chicago-Lambeth Quadrilateral. It is one of the proudest contributions of our church to international Anglicanism and to the ecumenical movement, rightly enshrined in the historical documents section of the 1979 prayer book. It was put forth by our House of Bishops in 1886, refined by the Lambeth Conference of 1888, and confirmed by the General Convention of 1895.

One of the four pillars of the Quadrilateral is Scripture, which not only contains all things needful for salvation but is also the "rule and ultimate standard of faith."[3] We can readily debate how to apply that

---

1 See R. William Franklin, "Conciliarism and the Ecclesiology of the Episcopal Church," *Sewanee Theological Review,* 61/2 (2018).

2 George R. Sumner, "Toward a more 'ecological' ecclesiology: Subsidiarity and conciliarism in context," *Sewanee Theological Review*, 61/2 (2018).

3 Lambeth Conference of 1888, Resolution 11, in The Book of Common Prayer (1979), 877.

rule to a contested issue. At just this point, conciliarism comes in. Each church has its own questions, related to its own cultural situation. But each needs to be open to the challenge of its sibling churches. Can they see this change as one consistent with the rule of faith? Can they recognize it as a legitimate development? In the last generation, the great missionary bishop Lesslie Newbigin eloquently articulated this sense of give and take between global churches.[4] Exegesis of Scripture, global communication, and the mission of God intersect. For Anglicans, the Book of Common Prayer serves as our spiritual and liturgical habitat for Scripture, creed, episcopacy, and the sacramental life. Across many differences in the Communion, this habitat is shared, as the space within which we consider doctrinal disagreement.

Perhaps the ever-present possibility of doctrinal contestation in a Communion based on both autonomy and interdependence should not surprise us. We do hear voices, however, that object to the status quo. On the one hand, some resist the fact that Anglican churches are "indeed independent," in the words of the 1920 Lambeth Conference—albeit, as the sentence continues, "independent with the Christian freedom which recognises the restraints of truth and love. They are not free to deny the truth. They are not free to ignore the fellowship."[5] On the other hand, if *doctrine* and *communion* are essential constituents of Anglicanism, then those who may wish to ignore this side of things are also paddling upstream. The trial verdict of Bishop Walter Righter in the 1990s concluded that the Episcopal Church

---

4 See, for example, *The Gospel in a Pluralist Society* (London: SPCK, 1989), ch. 15.

5 Quoted in *The Windsor Report* §86.

had no doctrines other than the core doctrine of the gospel, making it hard for a freelancing bishop to run afoul of anything. The recent experience of Bishop William Love of Albany tells a different story on this count.[6] Likewise, I have heard fellow Episcopal bishops say that, to them, communion is what they have experienced with churches where they serve, which they get to know. This is fair enough. But the level of provinces, gatherings of bishops, official liturgies, and the communications back and forth between them also embody our life in Christ. The rich word *communion* needs to cover all of this, and still more.

DEVELOPING DOCTRINE

Just here, we may wish to articulate a doctrine about contested doctrine, for which John Henry Newman will be helpful.[7] Newman was a traditional theologian, to say the least, but also acutely aware of modern questions about history and cultural relativity. How can a tradition remain the same if it changes? How can we grow and yet remain ourselves?

A word of background is in order. The final step in Newman's migration from the Church of England to Rome took place in 1845, when he also published his *Essay on the Development of Christian*

6　See Communion Partners, "Support for Bishop Love" (Oct. 10, 2020), available online at communionpartners.org. The Anglican Church of Canada's *St. Michael Report* (2005) helpfully distinguished doctrines which, while not themselves "core," imply and affect the latter.

7　I am grateful to Bishop Whalon for kindly suggesting this tack, building on my prior piece (see note 2, above).

Doctrine. The question carried great personal weight to him. He came to realize that doctrines about purgatory and Mary had changed over time, thus a straightforward Anglican primitivism, reaching back to the era of the undivided Church, would not suffice. But one also had to reckon with sheer historicist change. As a work by a newly minted Roman Catholic, Newman's *Essay* works backward from the solution of papal authority. But the central question was pertinent to theologians of all traditions: by what criteria might one discern whether a proposed development is legitimate? Newman was feeling his way and offering something less than a proof—rather more a direction, indicating how to proceed in a warranted way. The question recurs in every generation of the Church, with respect to one and another doctrine.

Here is Newman's argument, in brief. A bird is one with the egg, though looking very different. The bird never becomes a fish. How can something remain the same though appearing different? Here, Newman advises that we should avoid being "precisians," that is, ones who compulsively hold to every precise detail of the past. The question is what can change and what cannot. To answer we need criteria to discover genuine developments. Newman suggests seven criteria or tests, which he calls "notes."

The first criterion or note is *preservation of type*, which amounts to restating the challenge: the thing or matter in question needs to perdure recognizably over time.

Second is *continuity of principles*, by which Newman means the underlying logic of something. This requires doctrinal articulation and will amount to something more than simple replacement. Here Newman uses the metaphor of grammar, made famous a century and a quarter later by George Lindbeck of Yale.[8] It may take more time to discern what lies beneath than to form the doctrine: consider the early Church's centuries-long definition of the doctrine of the Trinity. This note remains too general to be much help, says Newman, since the reformer may simply produce a principle to suit the revision.

Thus, third, a *power of assimilation* is needed. Consider the way patristic theologians employed Greek philosophy to articulate Christian truth. The foreign idea may be molded to a new purpose or principle, but molded it must be, in a recognizably Christian way.

The fourth criterion is *logical sequence*, to show a trajectory of thought in which direction the novel doctrine may be found.

Fifthly, we need *anticipation of its future*. Early seeds of what would come later should already be in evidence.

Newman's sixth criterion for doctrinal development stipulates that it will *act conservatively upon its past*. By this he means that authentic developments are preceded by something similar, so that they do not "contradict and reverse the course of doctrine which has been developed before them, and out of which they spring." A corrupt development, by contrast, "ceases to illustrate, and begins to disturb, the acquisitions gained in its previous history" (*Essay* 5.6.1.).

Finally, an authentic development will display *chronic vigor*, that is, it will have staying power over time.

Well, if this all seems promising, we may wish to curb our

---

8   See George A. Lindbeck, *The Nature of Doctrine: Religion and Theology in a Postliberal Age*, 25th anniversary edn. with new intro. by Bruce D. Marshall and new afterword by author (Louisville: Westminster John Knox, 2009)

enthusiasm on several counts. Newman consciously assumed a magisterial context different from our own. Moreover, as Owen Chadwick has noted, organic metaphors such as *development* tend to want to "get to yes," as we say. Third, Newman's criteria are not ready-made to serve as umpire for our present disagreement over marriage. Progressives might valorize the criterion of *assimilation* with an eye to contemporary cultural consensus, while conservatives will note a lack of *anticipation* of the proposed development in earlier tradition.

Still, there is much of value in Newman's essay. The very idea of tests for our thinking together is useful, even if their implementation will invariably be contested. And Newman's anti-modern sense of time is both refreshing and critically necessary for contemporary Christians. In almost every case, doctrine develops over centuries, not decades. We need to cultivate a commitment to chronic continuance as a brake on our presentist impatience.

GUIDELINES FOR THE MOMENT

In the late 1980s I worked for Bishop Wes Frensdorff in the heyday of Canon-9 ordination in Navajoland. He liked to say that we were building the plane while we flew it. This is true also in the Anglican Communion: working out protocols as we try to implement them in the tensest of cases. It is not only *what* we shall decide about development that is conflicted, but *how* we do so. As a result—and harkening back to the sobering déjà vu with which we began—I would suggest that we are trying to discern something more modest than Newman, if aligned to his method and tenor. Let us call it *guidelines for the moment*. Such guidelines will help us maintain the highest degree of communion possible, a helpful phrase that emerged in discussions of the 1990s and helped to frame *The Windsor Report*. What might such guidelines look like?

I have four modest guidelines. I hope and believe they are in keeping with the spirit of Newman's project and can help contemporary Anglicans agree to a process of discerning potential doctrinal developments.

First, we must recognize that the redefinition of marriage is a contested doctrine; I have heard an Episcopal Church official call it "unsettled" with respect to the Communion, and that is true. I build here on the argument of Katherine Sonderegger in the preceding chapter of this volume. I don't mean only that the proposed redefinition is up in the air with our fellow churches, but that we recognize it to be so ourselves. This doesn't mean that progressives need to say they don't espouse it, nor lose the hope that it will one day be settled. It is a fact, however, that we still live with doctrinal disagreement between autonomous churches-in-communion, and indeed between distinct groups within our churches. In the Episcopal Church, we live with recent canonical changes and marriage liturgies for same-sex couples and with a preserved space for traditionally-minded dioceses, which are permitted to teach the former doctrine and observe the former discipline.

Second, as a result, the theological minority within our church, which still holds to the inherited teaching about marriage, has a special pertinence when it comes to our disagreements. As Christians, we rightly tend to various kinds of minorities, so there is an ecclesiological ethic in play here. We need the patience that Newman placed at the center of his proposal. A patiently pluralistic ecclesiology, making space for minorities out of respect and love, derives not only from a general sense of tolerance, but from a recognition of the nature of our living between autonomy and interdependence. This is the theological warrant for "communion across difference."

Third, disagreement over the proposed development of marriage has significant implications. Though all Anglican churches still share a great deal doctrinally, our disagreement here is intractable, with no sign of consensus with respect to Newman's fourth criterion, logical sequence. One option here is certainly a negotiated separation *tout court*, as the Anglican Church in North America and elements in the GAFCON movement have pressed, in one way and another, over the last decade. To date, however, the majority in the Communion has preferred to feel its way toward a continuing common life marked, for now (at least), by an elasticity. We have here, in *The Windsor Report* and elsewhere, helpfully spoken of degrees of communion, voluntary boundaries, and affinities. Though *covenant* has become for a time that which must not be named, the proposed Anglican Covenant of 2009 did helpfully imagine a voluntary coalition of the willing sans expulsion. It implied rather the differentiated definition of Communion toward which Archbishop Rowan Williams was pointing. Making space for productive or "good" disagreement, in Archbishop Welby's term, implies and in fact requires making space for several states of communion within a larger whole. This is not Newmanesque from his Roman period but seems to follow from the terms Newman set out prior to his departure.

Fourth and finally, we need to recognize that our Communion deals with the question of development at more levels than we sometimes admit. As ever, development is not an ethereal question but has real consequences for real communities. When the philosopher of religion William Christian wrote about the doctrines religious communities have concerning what he calls "alien claims," that is, the doctrines of other communities, he had in mind something like the Roman Catholic Church, where one can refer to Denzinger, or the catechism, and see the official teaching.9 The Anglican situation is more complicated—ecclesiologically, given our structural flux, and because of our diffuse sense of doctrine. Dioceses have relations to dioceses in other provinces, despite official differences that would seem to exclude such ties. Institutions of a more voluntary nature—seminaries, mission societies, renewal groups, and publications—play a role in the interstices, between the official churches, by loosening up the ground, cultivating friendships, and building trust. All of these create openings, mitigate conflict, and sow seeds for a hoped-for future. I read an editorial in *The Economist* at the time of Gene Robinson's consecration called "In praise of holy fudge."10 While I do not agree that unclarity and paralysis have served us well, I do think that a certain multi-level messiness can support the patience we need amid a Newman-style testing. Communion-amid-contest, at the margins and in creative spaces, including conferences and books, may provide a lubricant lest the gears seize up altogether.

9   See *Doctrines of Religious Communities: A Philosophical Study* (New Haven: Yale University Press, 1987).

10   *The Economist* (Nov. 6, 2003), available online.

EPISCOPALIAN HOPES

Where does this leave us? I speak from my own perspective, with an eye to the good of the Episcopal Church and the good of the Anglican Communion, in service of a larger Whole. The Communion Partners movement in North America, with which I am associated, has a Newmanesque role to play in the process of discernment amid doctrinal disagreement in the Anglican Communion.[11] Doctrinal developments, when they are legitimate, gain steam over time precisely as they are seen and accepted as developments rather than rejections of what has come before. If we take something like Newman's criteria of continuity, preservation, logical sequence, anticipation, and staying power to be correct, then we need traditional liturgies and the communities that practice them along the way of wise council, in order to reach consensus on the question at hand. For this reason, the Episcopal Church has done well to protect the "indispensable place that the minority who hold to this Church's historic teaching on marriage have in our common life, whose witness the Church needs."[12] Together, over time, Episcopalians of varying views can strive to do what all

---

11 See, e.g., our paper, "The Way of Anglican Communion: Walking Together before God" (May 2017), available online at communionpartners.org.

12 79th General Convention (2018), Resolution A227, which created the Task Force on Communion across Difference. The report of the task force should be required reading for all who care about the future of the Anglican Communion and its potential unity. See *"Put Out into the Deep Water": Communion across Difference as a Christian Call*, being a Report to the 80th General Convention of the Episcopal Church; available online in *The Blue Book 2021*.

Christians are called to do, with respect to marriage and every other question that arises, namely, assimilate all things—all truth, wherever it may be found—to the grammar of Christian belief, founded first and finally in holy Scripture. Along the way, we will need to answer objections and look for the fruits of the Spirit.

The Communion Partners remain resolved to serve as discursive colleagues and friends in Christ with all our siblings in the Episcopal Church, and to provide a point of contact with—and a bridge to— the Anglican Communion, the unity of which we are deeply devoted to encouraging and serving. May all the leaders of our church, and in the Communion, be enabled by God to press with joy into the common labor of teaching the faith clearly, courageously, charitably, and cooperatively, on the way to full communion, in God's good time.

THREE

Communion & Disagreement in Acts 15

Wesley Hill

One of the prominent themes for ongoing discussion and debate in the Episcopal Church at present is the theological status of moral disagreement. How are we to give a theological account of the fact of disagreement among Christians over moral issues, and how might we point the way toward its resolution or at least amelioration? The pitched battle for same-sex marriage (or marriage equality) rites has all but dissipated, at least in its most recent form, given the outcome of the 79th General Convention in 2018—which "memorialized" the 1979 Book of Common Prayer, thus guaranteeing that a traditional understanding of marriage as the union of male and female will remain available as one teaching, alongside the recently approved alternative marriage liturgies; and, via Resolution B012, made rites of marriage for same-sex couples available in every diocese and parish that wishes to use them, while providing a mechanism for traditionally-minded bishops to appropriate oversight of such parishes to another bishop. This truce of sorts, whereby two teachings about marriage sit uneasily alongside one another, seems to have lowered the temperature on at least one moral disagreement, though General Convention signaled a recognition that more theological work remains to be done by, for instance, commissioning a Task Force on Communion across Difference, the report of which was published in 2021.[1]

After long centuries, the divided churches of East and West are by now used to reflecting theologically on the status of doctrinal disagreement. But as Roman Catholic theologians Michael Root and James J. Buckley have pointed out, we are much less sure of the status of moral disagreement:

> While doctrinal issues have often in the past been the most ecumenically neuralgic topics, increasingly today ethical issues—abortion and homosexuality most prominently—have become a focus of difference between the churches and of potentially splintering debate within churches. These issues are more laden with emotion than many traditional doctrinal disputes, but ecumenical discussions have yet to address them in detail. We have little sense of just

---

1 Task Force on Communion across Difference, *"Put Out into the Deep Water": Communion across Difference as a Christian Call*, being a Report to the 80th General Convention of the Episcopal Church; available online in *The Blue Book 2021*.

when and how ethical disputes rightly impact communion within and among the churches. When can we live together with difference over such matters, and when does unity in Christ require common teaching?[2]

In the context of the Episcopal Church and the wider Anglican Communion, work on what the Archbishop of Canterbury has called "good disagreement" has in many ways only just begun. The Church of England Conversations regarding sexuality in 2015-16 were forthright in acknowledging that theological reflection on moral disagreement was still in its infancy, and they postponed any possibility of a common mind on the matter for the foreseeable future, while calling for Christians to "consider together what the practical consequence of disagreement might be" and enjoining charity and Christlike humility in the process.[3]

As we Anglicans continue to engage the question of the theological status of moral disagreement in our own churches and ecumenically, one of our tasks is to return to Scripture for illumination and instruction. Just here, one particular scriptural text has recommended itself as especially germane in Anglican debates about sexuality. I refer to the account of the so-called "Jerusalem Council" in Acts 15, in which Peter, Barnabas, and Paul recount to James and the other

---

2 Michael Root and James J. Buckley, eds., *The Morally Divided Body: Ethical Disagreement and the Disunity of the Church*, The Pro Ecclesia Series (Eugene, OR: Cascade, 2012), ix.

3 Church of England, *Shared Conversations on Sexuality, Scripture and Mission* (GS Misc 1083, June 2014), available online.

Jerusalem apostles and elders the effects of their missionary proclamation of Jesus as Messiah among the Gentiles. That the Gentiles receive the Spirit apart from being circumcised and observing other dictates of the Mosaic law counts, says Peter, as certification that they are acceptable before God through Christ as they are and do not need to be circumcised in order to attain justified status (vv. 7-11). For many readers in recent decades, this text has suggested, by analogy, that there is warrant for the full inclusion of lesbian and gay couples in our churches, apart from their having to accept traditional heterosexual behaviors or mores.[4] Additionally, perhaps more for "traditionalist" or "conservative" readers, Acts 15 has loomed large in discussions of moral disagreement because of the manner of adjudicating such disagreement that it displays.[5]

In what follows my aim is not so much to relitigate these long-running exegetical and hermeneutical debates. I do not intend to provide new arguments for the "traditional" or "conservative" conclusion on

---

4   See especially Stephen E. Fowl, *Engaging Scripture: A Model for Theological Interpretation* (Oxford: Blackwell, 1998), 97-127; Luke Timothy Johnson, *Scripture and Discernment: Decision Making in the Church* (Nashville: Abingdon, 1996), 144-8; Sylvia C. Keesmaat, "Welcoming in the Gentiles: A Biblical Model for Decision Making" in Greig Dunn and Chris Ambridge, eds., *Living Together in the Church: Including Our Differences* (Toronto: Anglican Book Centre, 2004), 30-49.

5   In the words of the announcement for the present consultation ("When Churches in Communion Disagree") at Virginia Theological Seminary, Jan. 2020: "One defining feature of the Anglican Communion around the world is a shared commitment to decision-making by synod, in the model of the Council of Jerusalem described in Acts 15."

the moral status of same-sex relationships, with which I still agree.[6] What I will do instead is offer three theses—arising from exegetical engagement with and hermeneutical reflection on Acts 15—that, I propose, ought to help guide the appropriation of Acts 15 within the ongoing discernment of the theological status of moral disagreement. Put differently, I won't argue so much for one particular "side" in the disagreement over sexuality. I will argue for how I propose the two opposed sides ought to go about appealing to Acts 15 in the context of their disagreement.

❈ ❈ ❈

My first thesis is simple and preliminary, and I mean it mainly to be a defensive validation of the desire to turn to Acts 15 in this context: *The disagreement over the circumcision of Gentile converts is best understood as a genuine moral and theological disagreement.*

Modern historical consciousness, with its desire not to impose anachronistic schemata on ancient texts, has ironically not much helped us to grasp what is at stake in this text, insofar as it has trained us to approach Acts 15 as an example of a disagreement about "ceremony" or "ritualism" as opposed to "morality" or "theology."[7] For

6 My understanding of why "Gentile inclusion" cannot serve as a straightforward analogy for "lesbian and gay inclusion" today is largely compatible with that of Richard Hays in *The Moral Vision of the New Testament: A Contemporary Introduction to New Testament Ethics* (San Francisco: HarperSanFrancisco, 1996), 399. I will return to this matter briefly below.

7 Distinguishing between civil, ceremonial, and moral precepts in the Mosaic law goes back at least as far as Aquinas: "We must therefore

first-century Jews, however, the circumcision of the flesh was not disconnected from what we would call the moral or ethical life. Not only was circumcision commanded in the Mosaic law and thus part and parcel of what the law would describe as a life of obedience; it was also understood as the visible and effectual renunciation of the "evil impulse" that dominated Jewish understanding of temptation, moral struggle, and the quest for a life of virtue.[8] For the Jerusalem apostles to disagree with Paul and others about whether Gentile believers in Jesus as the Messiah needed to be circumcised is therefore properly characterized as a disagreement about moral behavior with theological, and not just sociological, ramifications. Thus Acts 15 is much more relevant to our current moral and theological disagreements than we might have initially thought.

Pauline scholar and Duke Divinity School professor Douglas Campbell captures the force of this point with a contemporary analogy:

> Imagine that an astonishingly successful mission suddenly explodes
> in Utah. Young ministers, graduates of Duke Divinity School and
> so highly trained in the importance of noncolonial sensibilities,

---

distinguish three kinds of precept in the Old Law; viz. 'moral' precepts, which are dictated by the natural law; 'ceremonial' precepts, which are determinations of the Divine worship; and 'judicial' precepts, which are determinations of the justice to be maintained among men" (*Summa theologiae* I-II, q. 99, a. 4).

8   On circumcision as the commencement of law observance and as the provision and empowerment for resisting the "Impulsive Desire of the Flesh," see J. Louis Martyn, *Galatians: A New Translation with Introduction and Commentary*, AB 33A (New York: Doubleday, 1997), 289-94.

have been sent there by the bishop of the eastern conference of North Carolina to do mission work, and people have begun to flood into the Methodist churches in and around Salt Lake City. The mission's success verges on being a revival. The bishop is initially very pleased. But then disturbing reports begin to reach her.

Apparently, these flocks of new converts all happily confess that Jesus is Lord and endorse the triune God of grace. But churchgoing with special linen undergarments is viewed as acceptable, if not as standard. Sayings from the book of Mormon are being quoted liberally in the church alongside quotations from the Bible. And most disturbing of all, there are rumors that polygamy has been ruled acceptable, and many male converts with multiple wives are coming tearfully out of the closet and living and worshiping openly with their impressively large families.

The bishop contemplates simply excommunicating the young missionaries and their new congregations immediately. But she generously sends a letter instead ordering all those involved to return to traditional Christian practices pending further consideration.

To her surprise, the missionaries involved confront her representatives very directly about these instructions and a heated public argument ensues. The orders, moreover, are rejected by these Utah missionaries in no uncertain terms, with copious quotations from Scripture and tradition in ostensible support of their radical departures. Fortunately, all the parties concerned subsequently agree to journey back to North Carolina to meet together to try to decide what should be done (before, that is, they go to general conference). They will seek the will of God together concerning this entire controversy.

> In just this sense but more so, Paul's Christian communities
> were a shockingly radical departure from standard Jewish practices.
> Many of the things that Jews hold most dear were not being taught
> and practiced. Small wonder that a delegation from Jerusalem
> sought to take matters in hand.[9]

This effectively illustrates the moral stakes of Acts 15. It is some-times said, among contemporary observers of moral disagreement among the divided churches, that we may find, at most, remote analogies in the New Testament for our current disagreements, since the New Testament's examples of disagreement concern matters of ritual purity or ceremony rather than ethical disagreement. But this anachronistically separates what would have been inseparable for the New Testament writers. The disagreement over the necessity of circumcision was, among other things, a moral disagreement, and thus Acts 15 is appropriately scrutinized here by us in the context of contemporary concern for the churches' moral disagreements.

❋ ❋ ❋

My second thesis relates to the much-discussed verdict that James renders in vv. 13-21. After Peter, Barnabas, and Paul complete their narrative recounting of how God performed signs and wonders through them among the Gentiles and bestowed the Spirit on the Gentiles without their having first gotten circumcised, James summarily

---

9   Douglas A. Campbell, *Pauline Dogmatics: The Triumph of God's Love* (Grand Rapids: Eerdmans, 2020), 481-2.

concludes: "Simeon has related how God first looked favorably on the Gentiles, to take from among them a people for his name. This agrees with the words of the prophets" (vv. 14-15).[10] However, as several readers have pointed out, this translation actually reverses what the Greek says: "with this the words of the prophets agree" (τούτῳ συμφωνοῦσιν οἱ λόγοι τῶν προφητῶν). Many who have sought warrant in Acts 15 for the inclusion of non-celibate LGBTQ believers in the Church today have placed enormous weight on the direction of James's formulation in the latter, more literal translation. For example, consider this comment from Luke Timothy Johnson:

> [James] says that "the prophets agree with this" rather than that "this agrees with the prophets" (15:15). In other words, it is the experience of God revealed through narrative which is given priority in this hermeneutical process: the text of Scripture does not dictate how God should act. Rather, God's action dictates how we should understand the text of Scripture.[11]

In other words, James appears to subordinate the inscripturated prophetic word to the missional experience of Peter, Barnabas, and Paul; which, in turn, for Johnson and others, warrants the subordination of the supposed scriptural prohibition of same-sex sexual intimacy to the experience of observable LGBTQ holiness and

---

10 All Scripture quotations, unless otherwise noted, are taken from the New Revised Standard Version (NRSV).

11 Luke Timothy Johnson, *The Acts of the Apostles*, Sacra Pagina (Collegeville, MN: Liturgical Press, 1992), 271.

acceptance in contemporary contexts.

Were this the only possible construal of the text, it would seem to forecast the settling of moral disagreement by one "side" of our current ecclesial division simply giving up its position and capitulating to the other side. Those who believe that they should not (or cannot) bless same-sex unions as Christian marriages would, like James, need to allow contemporary experience to override their prior understanding of Scripture and thus surrender their previous belief. Here, however, it is crucial to note that, while Johnson and others are correct that James reasons from the experiential testimony of Peter, Barnabas, and Paul back to the interpretation of the words of the prophets, he still treats the words of the prophets as abidingly authoritative. It is not so much that experience alters or reconfigures the scriptural word. It is that experience is treated as illuminative of the scriptural word, with Scripture retaining its authoritative role albeit in a newly unveiled form. Richard Hays makes the point forcefully:

> [T]he experience of uncircumcised Gentiles responding in faith to the gospel message led the church back to a new reading of Scripture. This new reading discovered in the texts a clear message of God's intent, from the covenant with Abraham forward, to bless all nations and to bring Gentiles (qua Gentiles) to worship Israel's God.... Only because the new experience of Gentile converts proved hermeneutically illuminating of Scripture was the church,

over time, able to accept the decision to embrace Gentiles within the fellowship of God's people.[12]

What Acts 15 envisages, in other words, is a more complex, dialectical and hermeneutical process, in which missionary experience sheds new light on Scripture and in which Scripture, in turn, validates or confirms what experience has taught. The party at the council in Jerusalem concerned to safeguard the scriptural deposit is not shown to be simply in the wrong. Their understanding of Scripture is, to be sure, transformed, but their basic commitment to scriptural authority is left intact. And this, finally, suggests my second thesis: *The search for reconciliation and unity of mind does not require either "side" in an*

---

12 Hays, *Moral Vision*, 399. Compare the remarks of Jason Byassee: "The reason [the analogy between Gentile inclusion in Acts 15 and lesbian and gay inclusion is flawed] is that the early Christians could look back on Jewish scripture and see, after the fact, a narrative logic by which the gentiles were intended from the beginning to be included in the covenant community with the dawning of the eschaton. There is no similar scriptural logic for the inclusion of lesbians and gays into the covenant community at the eschaton. If one could argue scripturally that the dawning of the eschaton with the church as its earnest should mean that homosexual persons (to be clear: those unrepentant of their sexual practices) should stream to Zion like gentile worshipers of the Lord, then the analogy can hold. As it stands, it seems the argument fails to be fitting with the words on the page of scripture" (*Praise Seeking Understanding: Reading the Psalms with Augustine* [Grand Rapids: Eerdmans, 2007], 147 n. 107). See also Christopher R. Seitz, "Dispirited: Scripture as Rule of Faith and Recent Misuse of the Council of Jerusalem: Text, Spirit, and Word to Culture," in *Figured Out: Typology and Providence in Christian Scripture* (Louisville: Westminster John Knox, 2001), 117-29.

intractable moral disagreement to surrender its conviction regarding what is good. What is required is a willingness to be led by the Spirit into new understandings that may recast, without necessarily overturning, previously held convictions.

This way of framing the quest for unity is commonplace in ecumenical theology, where rapprochement is often portrayed not as "minimizing intractable differences, nor [as] one side capitulating to the other, but rather [as] pushing forward to more complex and multidimensional soteriologies (and ecclesiologies) that can critically appropriate what is valid in opposing views."[13] Many theologians and ethicists have suggested that a similar posture ought to obtain when the churches face moral disagreements. Oliver O'Donovan has tied this approach to the churches' moral disagreement over human sexuality. As he writes:

> The only thing I concede in committing myself to … a process [of dialogue between "gay-affirming" Christians and "tradition-al" Christians] is that if I could discuss the matter through with an opponent sincerely committed to the Church's authorities, Scripture chief among them, the Holy Spirit would open up perspectives that are not immediately apparent, and that patient and scrupulous pursuit of these could lead at least to giving the problem a different shape—a shape I presume will be compatible with, though not precisely identical to, the views I now hold, but which may also be compatible with some of the views my opponent now

---

13 George Hunsinger, *Disruptive Grace: Studies in the Theology of Karl Barth* (Grand Rapids: Eerdmans, 2000), 14 n. 20.

holds, even if I cannot yet see how. I do not have to think I may be mistaken about the cardinal points of which I am convinced. The only thing I have to think—and this, surely, is not difficult on such a subject!—is that there are things still to be learned by one who is determined to be taught by Scripture how to read the age in which we live.[14]

Ephraim Radner, writing as an avowed conservative, has similarly defended the notion that we should walk with and learn from those with whom we disagree about questions of sexuality. "While it is hard for me to believe," he reflects,

> that there is some new truth yet to be revealed... that will overturn the basic traditions of the Church's doctrine, nonetheless we must acknowledge the possibility of still learning something we did not know before on the matter. And where else shall we learn this than with those who challenge us about our exhausted outlooks? A pertinent analogy is the experience and understanding of something like witchcraft, the debate around which in the seventeenth century led not only to a critical reassessment of the parameters of its practice and meaning, but also, interestingly enough, contributed to a fertile burst of exploration and insight into the physical sciences.... The basic teaching of the Church concerning the existence of the evil one and of evil in general did not change. But because of these debates, Christians now approach the question of witchcraft

---

14   Oliver O'Donovan, *Church in Crisis: The Gay Controversy and the Anglican Communion* (Eugene, OR: Cascade, 2008), 33.

very differently and much more circumspectly than in the sixteenth century. That is surely a blessing. Similarly, there is every reason to hope that God might lead us into some greater light around the issue of sexuality even in our era, a hope that properly demands an embodiment in patient listening and discussion, none of which need constitute an abandonment of our basic teaching.[15]

This is the posture Acts 15 encourages. Instead of prompting the question, "How can the other side be made to see things my way?" the text appears to suggest that both "sides" of a moral disagreement may find themselves transformed as they together engage the experiential and scriptural contours of their disagreement. The disagreement may or may not be thereby resolved, but it will almost certainly be given a more promising shape.

❋ ❋ ❋

Third and finally, *Acts 15 suggests that moral disagreement is enclosed within the missional, reconciling purpose of God and is superintended by the Spirit.*

When we attempt to draw connections between Acts 15 and our contemporary experience of moral disagreement, we should attend to the placement of the chapter in the larger narratival and theological structure of Acts as a whole. First, we have the opening frame: "In the first book, O Theophilus, I have dealt with all that Jesus began to

---

15 Ephraim Radner, *Hope Among the Fragments: The Broken Church and Its Engagement of Scripture* (Grand Rapids: Brazos, 2004), 53.

do and teach" (1:1, RSV; Τὸν μὲν πρῶτον λόγον ἐποιησάμην περὶ πάντων, ὦ Θεόφιλε, ὧν ἤρξατο ὁ Ἰησοῦς ποιεῖν τε καὶ διδάσκειν). This framing implies that what will follow in the narrative to come, in contrast to the earlier Gospel of Luke (which forms the first "volume" of what New Testament scholars tend to view as a two-volume work, "Luke-Acts"), is the record of what Jesus continues to do and teach. What Jesus continues to do and teach, after his ascension, through the agency of the poured-out Holy Spirit, surely includes the Lord's work in and through the vicissitudes, detours, and tensions of the Acts narrative.[16] And this providential work in the midst of conflict and brokenness is foregrounded when the opening of chapter 8 records the outcome of the persecution the believers in Jerusalem endure. As St. Luke says, "all except the apostles were scattered throughout the countryside of Judea and Samaria" (Acts 1:1). The violence the Church suffers is thus made to serve her mission, as Jesus had forecasted at the narrative's beginning: "you will be my witnesses in Jerusalem, in all Judea and Samaria, and to the ends of the earth" (1:8). Persecution leads to the fulfillment of Jesus's prediction. The Lord guides and governs even the narrative's most unassimilable elements, bending them to a higher purpose.

The same pattern holds with respect to chapter 15. The disagreement between the apostles over the status of uncircumcised Gentiles becomes the doorway into the second missionary journey of Paul, leading to evangelism in Macedonia and elsewhere. The conflict among the apostles was not ancillary to this outcome. It was ingredient to it.

---

16 Hays, *Moral Vision*, 112.

This suggests, I believe, that we must do more than merely ask about the theological status of moral disagreement and how to go about achieving unity of mind and spirit among contemporary believers. We must also inquire into what we might call, with a nod to Ephraim Radner,[17] a pneumatology of moral disagreement. We "cannot be satisfied with an account of Christian division which fails to say what God has to do with it."[18] Acts 15 suggests that our task is not merely to strategize an end to moral disagreement but also to probe, amid ongoing disagreement, what God's strange purposes might be in permitting believers to remain at odds with one another over moral matters (cf. 1 Cor. 11:19).

Such an inquiry should not lead to theological fatalism. We should not use the Spirit's ability to work in and through human recalcitrance and folly as an excuse to rest content with disagreement, throwing up our hands and declaring that it must be God's will for us since we cannot find a way beyond it. But nor should we fail to recognize that the Spirit can make use of human conflict as well as concord. The command to maintain unity of Spirit, even in its breach, *will* be caught up in the Spirit's work of judgment and purgation. How might our moral disagreement appear in a new light if we ask, through prayer, study, and debate, how God is acting in, through, and beyond it?

---

17   See Ephraim Radner, *The End of the Church: A Pneumatology of Christian Division in the West* (Grand Rapids: Eerdmans, 1998).

18   Bruce D. Marshall, "Review Essay: The Divided Church and Its Theology," *Modern Theology* 16/3 (2000): 377-396, at 381.

※ ※ ※

I have not sought here to propose concrete resolution of current moral disagreements afflicting Episcopalians and Anglicans—disagreements that, of course, similarly afflict all Christians and churches, to one degree or another. Rather, I want us simply to see that a text as supposedly distant from our situation as Acts 15 can and does speak across the ages (as does, in fact, the entire canon of Scripture, New and Old). Precisely as it presents us with a situation of Christian moral and theological disagreement, proposes a broad and generous model of conciliarity, and narrates its conflict under the sign of a dark yet benevolent missionary divine providence, Acts 15 holds out hope for the Church today, which is the same Church of its own subject, the one holy catholic apostolic; yes, and also divided and disagreeing: the Church of the risen Lord Jesus Christ.

FOUR

Mapping Communion and Disagreement Ecclesiologically

Jeremy Worthen

PERSONS IN RELATION

What is the relation between communion and disagreement? In its widest sense, communion denotes a mode of relationship of persons defined by what they hold in common, that which exists *between* them. Disagreement is an action that takes place among persons and may disrupt their confidence in the commonality that constitutes this mode of relationship. Disagreement as thus defined, however, cannot be considered in isolation from agreement as the action that articulates such commonality and establishes confidence in its reality.

Disagreement marks the limit of agreement, its frustration, and is defined by that limit. Cliché aside, it is not possible to disagree with another person about everything. Only because we agree on some substantial parameters—including description of the subjects we are considering, moral limits in our communication with one another, and persuasive reasoning—can we conduct a disagreement at all, rather than a mere exchange of force or incomprehension. Disagreement therefore relies on some commonality, on some relationship of communion between the persons who are disagreeing.

As such, disagreement arises within communion from the desire for fuller agreement as the action that both expresses and sustains communion in human relationships. In cases where we do not see agreement as important for the relationship of communion between us, no disagreement need arise, only the recognition of mutually acceptable difference. Because agreement is therefore always the horizon for disagreement, disagreement not only threatens the relationship of interpersonal communion but also affirms it as one which ought to be expressed and confirmed in agreement. In this way, disagreement also paradoxically creates space for new actions of agreement that may extend the expression of that which is in common between us and thereby deepen our communion with one another. It is not as if there is some fixed quantity of propositions that we might affirm together, such that the more numerous are those on which we agree, the fewer will be those on which we disagree, and vice versa. On the contrary, new levels of agreement may open up new depths of disagreement, as they open up new horizons of understanding for our exploration. Similarly, disagreement may become an opportunity to move towards fuller and more transformative agreement.

The dynamic interactions between agreement and disagreement mark and drive the mode of our relationships of communion as human persons. Actions of agreement can generate and affirm that which is in common between us and therefore situate our communion with one another, just as actions of disagreement can interrupt and limit the expression of that communion. While they may thereby cause us to doubt the reliability of our communion, they can also drive us to renewed reflection on it that results in fresh appreciation and appropriation of that which we hold in common. To be in relationship as social creatures in time, human beings must be able to affirm agreement on some things while also bearing the experience of disagreement on others, not seeking to erase it by force but rather being ready to grasp the potential it carries for drawing us into deeper understanding, and therefore more complete agreement and fuller communion.

VISIBLE COMMUNION BETWEEN CHURCHES

The theology of communion is a substantial subject.[1] In the New Testament, those who believe in the good news of Christ have him in common, and therefore are in communion with one another and

---

1   See e.g. John Zizioulas, *Being as Communion* (Crestwood, New York: St. Vladimir's Seminary Press, 1985) and *Communion and Otherness: Further Studies in Personhood and Church*, ed. Paul McPartlan (London: T & T Clark, 2006); Nicholas Sagovsky, *Ecumenism, Christian Origins, and the Practice of Communion* (Cambridge: Cambridge University Press, 2000).

with God by *sharing in* Christ.[2] To believe in him is inseparable from life in him (as St. Paul insists), remaining in him (in St. John's language), and following him (as all the gospels display). In terms of Christian doctrine, the primary meaning of communion is the relationship of human persons with one another and with the eternal persons of the triune God that unfolds from sharing in the person and work of Jesus Christ.

To speak of communion *between churches*, rather than communion between persons in the Church, or the communion between persons that makes the Church, is thus to use the language of communion in a secondary and derivative way. We Anglicans have grown accustomed to this secondary, inter-ecclesial usage of *communion* in the last two centuries. In the classic texts of the 1920 Lambeth Conference, we see the primary communion of Christians in the Church described as "fellowship," while capital-C *Communion* is reserved for that which multiple churches share.[3] The two meanings are obviously interconnected but not identical.

---

2 See Church of England Faith and Order Commission, *Communion and Disagreement* (2016), §26: "As the first chapter of 1 John explains, the life of the church is defined by the intersection and inseparability between 'our fellowship... with the Father and with his Son Jesus Christ' (1 John 1:3) and our 'fellowship with one another' (1 John 1:7). It is not possible to have one without the other. 2 John spells out the corollary of this: if someone comes to adhere to a form of teaching that prevents fellowship with the Son, fellowship with them in the body of Christ cannot continue unimpeded either." Text available online.

3 For a full collection of the documents of the 1920 Lambeth Conference, see Randall Davidson, ed., *The Six Lambeth Conferences, 1867–1920* (London: SPCK, 1929).

In Catholic Christianity in the early centuries, and (with some differences) in the Orthodox and Roman Catholic churches today, the distinction between interpersonal and inter-ecclesial communion is not so sharply drawn. Members of different Catholic or Orthodox churches—in various geographical locales and jurisdictions—are understood simply as members of the one Church because they share a "fullness" of faith and life. They are in communion with one another in the Church on the same basis that they are in communion with others in their "particular" church, namely, by sharing in Christ.[4] Here also, however, the need for an account of communion *between* churches—beyond the communion of the one Church that includes all churches—arises as we start to wonder whether one plus one always equals one (as well as two) in our ecclesial arithmetic. This is the work of ecumenism: to wrestle with realities of division and the lack of "full communion" between churches that nonetheless profess some shared bond of faith with those from whom they are, to varying degrees, divided.

For our part, Anglicans traditionally have insisted *both* that our churches are part of the one catholic Church *and* that, added together, they do not constitute a single, Anglican Church. One can explain this irreducible plurality in terms of a historic Anglican aversion to forms of universal authority in the Church, together with a theological instinct that *Church* should carry with it specific expectations regarding authority and oversight. Our accustomed Anglican way of thinking and speaking also follows directly from the historical

---

4 See Christopher Ruddy, *The Local Church: Tillard and the Future of Catholic Ecclesiology* (New York: Crossroad Publishing, 2006).

intertwining of the roots of the Anglican Communion with the roots of the ecumenical movement. Lambeth Conferences up until at least the mid-twentieth century understood Anglican churches as first and foremost *part* of the Catholic Church *in their nation* or country. Accordingly, the communion between Anglican churches across national boundaries must be different from the union that should exist *visibly* between Anglican churches and every other part of Christ's Church in every single and specific place.[5]

In this classically Anglican perspective, "our" Communion of churches becomes both a passing sign and a potential instrument of the one communion in Christ that should bind together—again, visibly—all the united, catholic churches in every place. In this view, the Anglican Communion in no way serves as a substitute for local union. Communion between parts of Christ's body in different places, however salutary, does not obviate the call to unity with all Christians and churches in each place. For this reason, we have, as a global communion of churches, avoided the term *Anglican Church*. There are only local Anglican churches seeking the visible unity throughout the world of the one Catholic Church. When that goal is attained it will indeed be true to describe the plurality of united churches in communion with one another in every place as just that: the one Catholic Church.[6] At that point, the need to separate inter-ecclesial from interpersonal communion will fall away, as the differences between

---

5 Jeremy Worthen, "The Ecclesiology of Visible Unity at Lambeth 1920: Lost beyond Recovery?" in *Ecclesiology*, 16/2 (2020), 224-242.

6 Lambeth Conference 1920, Resolution 9, "Appeal to All Christian People," §I, available online.

particular churches will no longer inhibit the making visible of the unity between all who share together in the one Lord Jesus Christ.

Even as we seek visible Christian unity, Anglican churches remain bound to one another with strong and distinctive bonds that merit the description "Communion." In fact, the pattern of our life together in communion resembles the shape of our ecumenical labor—from local unions with other churches, like the united churches of South Asia, beginning with the formation of the Church of South India (in 1947), to inter-ecclesial communion, like that with the Old Catholic Churches of the Union of Utrecht (from 1931), or the agreement between the Episcopal Church and the Evangelical Lutheran Church in America (in 2000). It's hard to overstate the significance of the fact that the Chicago-Lambeth Quadrilateral (of 1886 and 1888) began life as a goad to local ecumenism but quickly came to function as an enduring outline of Anglican identity. The close connection has perhaps grown weaker in the last fifty years, but the Anglican Covenant of 2009 still spoke of a distinctly "ecumenical vocation" of Anglicanism.[7]

In the end, Anglican self-reflection about our own communion cannot help but shape how we relate to other Christian churches, and vice versa. As we seek to sustain interpersonal and inter-ecclesial communion as Anglicans and to deepen communion with others, the same call to visible Christian unity may be heard. This call, from Jesus himself, invites us to look away from our own interests and identities

---

7   Jeremy Worthen, "The Centenary of the 'Appeal to All Christian People' and the Ecumenical Vocation of Anglicanism," *Theology*, 123/2 (2020), 104-112. Cf. *God Wills Fellowship: Lambeth Conference 1920 and the Ecumenical Vocation of Anglicanism*, ed. Christopher Wells and Jeremy Worthen (Dallas: Living Church Books, 2022).

to that which we share in him, namely, "one Lord, one faith, one baptism, one God and Father of all, who is above all and through all and in all" (Eph. 4:5-6).

ECUMENICAL PRELIMINARIES

The ecumenical task has not been characteristically framed in terms of agreement and disagreement, but rather in the language of unity and diversity. With regard to the ecumenical movement, that language can be tracked for over a century, from the "Appeal to All Christian People" issued by the Lambeth Conference of 1920 to the convergence text on ecclesiology published by the World Council of Churches' Faith and Order Commission in 2013, *The Church: Towards a Common Vision*.[8] Its origins, however, reach much further back than that. The plea of Irenaeus of Lyons in the second century that the diversity between churches in different places on the dating for the celebration of Easter need not impair the unity between them demonstrates the antiquity of reflection along these lines.

Agreement and disagreement are not, however, simply synonyms for unity and diversity in this context. As noted above, agreement and disagreement are actions of and between persons who are in a relationship of communion with one another by virtue of what is

---

8   Lambeth Conference 1920, Resolution 9, "Appeal to All Christian People," §IV, in Davidson, ed., *Six Lambeth Conferences*; World Council of Churches Commission for Faith and Order (WCC), *The Church: Towards a Common Vision*, Faith and Order Paper 214 (Geneva: World Council of Churches, Commission on Faith and Order, 2013), §30: both available online.

common between them. Some people agree or disagree with some other people, and these actions have the potential to change the relationship of communion that currently exists, positively and negatively. Unity and diversity are states of affairs. These people are the same as one another in some respects, and different from one another in other respects. The distinction is important. It may be true that unity of practice in the life of the Church always implies some agreement, insofar as that practice carries theological meaning. That said, the same practice may be associated with different theological meanings in different churches. The bitter controversies of the Reformation period over the theology of the Eucharist provide a salutary example. Moreover, unity of practice may arise from or give rise to an overt act of agreement—that by doing this same thing, we are affirming the same meaning; but equally it may not. There is therefore a proper ecumenical question about occasions where unity as a state of affairs should be accompanied by the action of agreement in order to articulate or deepen communion; occasions, that is, where the action of agreement may be needed in order for the bare fact of commonality in forms of practice and belief to be grasped as unity in Christ.

On the other hand, it is certainly not true that diversity always implies some disagreement. In all kinds of human relationships, we accept that others are not the same as us; we expect diversity and treat it as normal. The sharp challenges for Christian unity, from the New Testament down to the present day, have always been about diversities of ecclesial practice and theological language that give rise to the activity of disagreement, and from that generate conflict and division. One form of response to such situations is to argue—as Irenaeus did with the date of Easter—that the diversity in question is part of the *legitimate* diversity that is to be expected in the Church as it fulfils its purpose of making disciples of all nations, bringing every culture, every time, and every unique human person into communion in Christ. Another form of response is to argue—as Irenaeus did with the self-described teachers of secret knowledge—that the diversity is *not* legitimate: that disagreement is in fact required of faithful believers and that if some will not agree with the truth that is taught in the Church then they may ultimately need to become separated from its life.[9]

The crucial difference between accepting diversity of theologically freighted practice as a state of affairs that has no bearing on our communion in Christ and identifying in it a disagreement that in some way questions that communion is that in the latter case the diversity is interpreted as a failing to agree, where agreement is an action we ought to be able to make in expressing and confirming our common life in Christ. Unless there is some sense of agreement on this matter as the proper accompanying action for our relationship of communion, then disagreement between churches about it only needs to be unmasked as a mistaken fussiness about diversity. Its substance can be safely set to one side. In ecumenical relations as in human relationships generally, we cannot understand our disagreements without beginning to articulate the corresponding agreements we think we ought to be able to make by virtue of the communion that exists between us.

As was proposed by the Church of England's Faith and Order

---

9 Loveday Alexander and Morwenna Ludlow, "Irenaeus and the Date of Easter," in *Supporting Papers for the Faith and Order Commission Report, Communion and Disagreement*, 2016, 19–28; available online.

Commission in its report on *Communion and Disagreement*, long-lasting and divisive disagreements in the history of the Church have tended to be marked by disagreement as to which of these two responses is required: Irenaeus' approach to different dates for celebrating Easter, or his approach to different teachings about the knowledge that comes from faith in Christ.[10] Already with the trinitarian controversies of the 4th century, the entanglement can be observed of disagreement on the presenting theological issues with disagreement as to whether difference of liturgical language can be read as legitimate diversity, or otherwise marks a failing to express agreement in communion—in which case the disagreement must be faced on the way to re-establishing the agreement of communion. Differences between churches over the baptism of infants since the 16th century provide another example here. Christians who take the same position on the substantial question of whether infants should be baptised may still disagree with one another as to whether it is possible to accept differing approaches on this matter. Different missional and pastoral priorities may lead to varying estimations about the resilience of communion within and between churches, and about whether this is a matter that requires doctrinal agreement in all times and all places for communion to be sustained (as the 16th-century Reformers on all sides of the debate generally assumed it did).

In contemporary ecumenism, this compounding of two different levels of disagreement—about both the subject of the disagreement and its theological status—may also be present, though not necessarily in such an obvious way. One of the critical issues in many

10   Faith and Order Commission, *Communion and Disagreement*, §§53–65.

attempts to move towards ecclesial communion between Anglican churches and Protestant churches has been the expectation enshrined in both the Chicago-Lambeth Quadrilateral and the 1920 "Appeal to All Christian People" that sharing together in the historic episcopate is necessary for visible unity. What does it mean for a church that does not understand its exercise of *episcopé* in the precisely Anglican terms of "the historic episcopate" to consider receiving the latter? Is it enough for the church in question to have some people ordained to a role that is recognizable to Anglicans as episcopal, by people Anglicans can recognize as bishops standing in the historic episcopate? If so, is this because such matters of Church order are essentially *adiaphora*, to be settled as seems best for the sake of unity in mission? Or is it necessary that the church in question recognize the historic episcopate as God's providential gift to the universal Church, integral to the *bene* or *plene esse* of the church, if not its *esse* as such? Put another way: is it possible for a church to receive the historic episcopate without valuing it within in its own ecclesiology? There is clearly a case to be made for responding in the negative. But the theological value of the historic episcopate is also a matter of dispute among Anglicans, so it seems unreasonable to insist on agreement between Anglican and other churches not only on grounds of practical church order but also theological status. Yet subject and status, here as in so many other cases, cannot be neatly separated. *Historic episcopate* is not simply a historical or phenomenological description but implies a kind of ecclesiological weight, perhaps difficult to define.

Differences of ecclesiology could be said to characterize the space within which ecumenism operates. Different churches, and different global Communions, are to some extent defined over against one another by their ecclesiological differences. That is not to say that the only area for greater agreement for the sake of fuller communion, and therefore the only area for disagreement, is ecclesiology. Yet differences of ecclesiology bring with them different assumptions about how ecclesial agreement is to be articulated and confirmed. This brings the accompanying risk in ecumenical dialogue that one church may not be able to receive the agreement of another because it is not offered in its own native or habituated ecclesial register, leading to the conclusion that disagreement continues. Such differences in how agreement is to be normatively expressed by churches risk further complicating the experience of disagreement in ecumenical encounter, as I will discuss further in the next section.

In the light of these initial observations, what kind of relations exist in the context of ecumenical endeavour between inter-ecclesial communion and doctrinal agreement and disagreement? At least three connected types of relation might be noted. First, there is agreement that articulates the reality of communion between the members of one church and the members of another, by which they recognize one another as members of the one body of Christ and, perhaps, seek fuller communion. Correspondingly, there is disagreement that may jeopardise such communion between the members of different churches. Second, there is agreement that enables that communion to be expressed in various forms of common action, including sharing in worship, witness, and discipleship. Correspondingly, there is disagreement that obstructs the expression of communion in action. Third, there is agreement that becomes newly possible because churches are in communion, and disagreement that prevents such agreement from happening.

(1) AGREEMENT THAT ARTICULATES COMMUNION, DISAGREEMENT THAT UNDERMINES IT

Agreements that articulate the reality of communion between members of distinct churches is foundational for the ecumenical movement. If communion with others in the life of the Church is a divine gift that cannot be separated from receiving Christ in faith by baptism, then acts of agreement in that faith place us in a relationship of deepening communion with one another, even if barriers and estrangements between our churches still persist. In this way, the theological reality of common life in Christ becomes a foundation for relations between different churches on which to build towards fuller communion. Or, to put it another way, the divine gift of communion generates an imperative for human beings to seek the fullness of communion in our churches as social bodies whose unity should be visible to the world as sign, instrument, and foretaste of the gospel of reconciliation. Obversely, difficulties in enacting agreement in the faith by which we receive Christ sow doubts as to whether some churches truly enable people to receive Christ at all, thus undermining the basis for ecumenical endeavour and implying that relations need to be placed in a different category.

As noted toward the end of the previous section, one challenge here for ecumenical endeavour concerns how agreement in the faith by which we are made one with and in Christ is to be enacted by participating churches. One might consider, for instance, the first paragraph of the "basis" of the World Council of Churches: "The World Council of Churches is a fellowship of churches which confess the Lord Jesus

Christ as God and Saviour according to the scriptures, and therefore seek to fulfil together their common calling to the glory of the one God, Father, Son and Holy Spirit." *Fellowship*—that is, communion—is linked to *confession*, which is in this context the action of agreement on theological truth. In the original constitution of the WCC in 1948, this sentence referred to "our" Lord Jesus Christ, ended with "Saviour," and used the verb "accept" rather than "confess." Within a few years this attracted criticism, which led to the current formulation, approved at the General Assembly in New Delhi in 1961.[11]

The changes indicate several significant issues. First, accepting—receiving—Christ needs to be enacted and communicated by confessing him, that is, by a formal and public agreement that he is God and Saviour. Second, such agreement needs to make it clear that our understanding of him as God and Saviour is "according to the scriptures," that is, faithful to them. Third, such agreement in common faith commits us to common action. Fourth, to understand our faith and our calling, we are bound to name God as Trinity: Father, Son, and Holy Spirit. If a given group of Christians, therefore, does not formally confess Christ as God and Saviour, does not hold its doctrine to be accountable to the teaching of Scripture, and does not name God as Trinity, it cannot be part of this fellowship of churches. The WCC might not say so, but we could conclude that, theologically, such a group would not be part of the communion of churches constituted by agreement in the faith by which we are joined to Christ and therefore joined to one another in Christ.

11   See the World Council of Churches website, "The Basis of the WCC," available online.

This one example perhaps suffices to highlight some of the difficulties that may arise at this point. Confessing Christ "as God," together with the naming of God as Trinity, will invoke for many the Nicene Creed, as the Chicago-Lambeth Quadrilateral had done. Historic differences between churches about the use of creeds and confessions would have prevented the WCC from simply referring to it at this point, though a concerted attempt was subsequently made to explore the extent to which it could serve as a common form of words for "confessing the faith" of all member churches.[12] What is the role of creeds here, especially in a context in which, since the 19th century, many in positions of teaching authority in mainline churches have openly questioned certain creedal claims, including the divinity of Christ?

The phrase "according to the scriptures" signals a different though not unrelated set of questions. To what extent does it imply agreement on an understanding of the authority of Scripture, such that a theological approach deemed to undermine that authority, even in areas that do not have a direct bearing on the matter of the creeds, is also bound to undermine the capacity of churches to "confess the Lord Jesus Christ as God and Saviour according to the scriptures," and therefore to be in fellowship with one another at all? Disagreement on such points unsettles confidence that we can begin dialogue between different churches from a position of communion with one another in Christ.

---

12 World Council of Churches' Commission on Faith and Order, *Confessing One Faith: Towards an Ecumenical Explication of the Apostolic Faith as Expressed in the Nicene-Constantinopolitan Creed (381)* (Geneva: World Council of Churches, Commission on Faith and Order, 1987).

One other matter raised in the previous section is also worth underlining at this point. Agreements and disagreements that bear on communion are bound to have an ecclesiological dimension. That is not because they must concern the doctrine of the Church as their subject. In this first type of relation between communion, agreement, and disagreement they normally do not. In the second type, they sometimes will; in the third, it is inherent that they should. The issue here is that agreement and disagreement in this context are ecclesial actions whereby a church communicates its definitive understanding. Examples of such actions include the foundational commitments that define a church's polity, its norms of public worship, and decisions made by bodies and individuals that hold oversight and authority. In order to be the kind of agreement or disagreement that carries weight for determining the relation that obtains between churches, it must be recognizable as the action of those churches, and the question of what enables such recognizability is an ecclesiological question. To return to the example just given, a church in which baptism in the name of the Trinity is understood theologically as the basis for membership, with baptismal candidates expected to declare their faith using the Apostles' Creed and to become regular participants in the Eucharist where the Nicene Creed will normally be recited, could be said to enact its agreement with the basis of the WCC through a sacramental practice in which all share. This point is also relevant to the second and third types of agreement and disagreement as described below.

(2) AGREEMENT THAT ENABLES
THE EXPRESSION OF COMMUNION,
DISAGREEMENT THAT OBSTRUCTS IT

The issue of who belongs within the fellowship of churches, and how the line should be drawn around it, is one that ecumenism cannot entirely avoid, not least in the case of what are sometimes called ecumenical instruments, such as the WCC, that will regularly receive membership applications. Nonetheless, most ecumenical work at an institutional level over the past century has taken place between churches that accept the reality of a relationship of communion existing between them based on their agreement in the faith by which they are joined in Christ, often associated with baptism. On this basis, they recognize themselves as having a shared responsibility and duty to make the communion that flows from the reconciling work of Christ visible to the world for which he died. The challenge here has been about how that communion can be expressed in common action, including sharing together in worship, sacraments, service, and mission, where these depend in part on our ability to accept one another's members and ministers as free to act across the borders of our churches.[13] To some extent, we can map across here to the third element of the Chicago-Lambeth Quadrilateral, as we could in the

---

13 For this understanding of common action and common life, see William Adam, Matthias Grebe, and Jeremy Worthen, "The Church of England and European Ecumenism: Making our Unity Visible" in *After Brexit? European Unity and the Unity of European Churches*, ed. Matthias Grebe and Jeremy Worthen (Leipzig: Evangelische Verlagsanstalt, 2019), 129–48.

preceding section to the first and second, although the correspondence in this case is more limited. Sacraments are only one form of common action expressing participation in our common life in Christ—though one might well argue they have a distinctive place of primacy among such actions.

Some of the most significant ecumenical texts since the 1970s represent attempts to set out agreement on areas of doctrine between churches that recognise the reality of communion between them, in the hope that this will enable growth towards fuller, more visible communion, not least in a shared sphere of action. Included in this category are 1981's *Final Report* of the first Anglican Roman Catholic International Commission (ARCIC); *Baptism, Eucharist and Ministry*, published in 1982 by the World Council of Churches' Faith and Order Commission; and the *Joint Declaration on the Doctrine of Justification*, originally signed by the Lutheran World Federation and the Roman Catholic Church in 1999, with three other world communions now associating themselves with it. All three texts have drawn levels of formal support that are exceptional for ecumenical statements.

Some differences may also be noted between these texts in terms of how they handle the relationship between agreement and disagreement. The original intention of ARCIC had been simply to present "agreed statements" on "The Eucharist" (1971), "Ministry and Ordination" (1973), and "Authority in the Church" (1976). These statements were only a few pages long, though they bore a great deal of weight as they sought to recover creatively the theological language of Scripture and the early Christian centuries. In this way, they hoped to set out what Anglicans and Roman Catholics could say together in a common form of words that bypassed the polemical exchanges and oppositional formulations characterizing the immediately preceding 500 years. Yet their reception in the Anglican Communion and the Catholic Church inevitably involved people asking how what was said in them related to the familiar oppositional formulations that had come to define both culture and teaching to a significant extent. On this count, each agreed statement required an "Elucidation" that could compete for length with the original statement and, in the case of "Authority in the Church," needed a further statement of its own.[14]

The interplay of agreement and disagreement appeared in a different form in *Baptism, Eucharist and Ministry*.[15] Here, areas of disagreement were highlighted within the original text, rather than addressed subsequently and separately, as in the first phase of ARCIC. The book was printed in two columns, with "commentary" material sometimes appearing in the right-hand column in italic type that noted continuing disagreements among the WCC's member churches in relation to the matter under consideration. Meanwhile, the content in normal type represented an approach, similar to ARCIC's, of seeking to distil statements on which churches could agree through creative recovery of sources common to all. As with ARCIC, Scripture was central and determinative, but the witness of the early centuries also played a crucial role—as, for instance, with the acceptance of both infant baptism and the postponement of baptism to adult years as commensurate with Christian tradition, or again, the commendation

---

14   ARCIC, *The Final Report* (1981), available online.

15   WCC Commission on Faith and Order, *Baptism, Eucharist and Ministry*, Faith and Order Paper 111 (1982), available online.

of the threefold order of ministry. As the designation of "convergence text" implied, *Baptism, Eucharist and Ministry* sought to convey the extent of potential agreement while also acknowledging continuing disagreements that would need to be addressed in due course.

The *Joint Declaration on the Doctrine of Justification* shows both continuity with and development from these earlier texts. Again, we have the fundamental methodology of seeking to fashion a concise statement, inspired by common sources, to which both communions can agree. In this case, the initial statement comprises three paragraphs only, followed by a further paragraph on the significance of the doctrine of justification for Lutherans and Catholics. It is introduced by the assertion that

> the Lutheran churches and the Roman Catholic Church have together listened to the good news proclaimed in Holy Scripture. This common listening, together with the theological conversations of recent years, has led to a shared understanding of justification. This encompasses a consensus in the basic truths; the differing explications in particular statements are compatible with it.[16]

This brief section summarising the consensus is then followed by a much lengthier one comprising seven sub-sections on specific topics pertaining to the doctrine of justification. Each of these is made up of three paragraphs, the first of which sets out a statement for agreement by Catholics and Lutherans on the topic, before the second and third

---

16 Lutheran World Federation and the Catholic Church, *Joint Declaration on the Doctrine of Justification* (1999), §14; available online.

comment on the distinctive approaches taken by Catholics and then Lutherans, or Lutherans and then Catholics (the order varies). The question of how far these "differing explications" constitute theological disagreements that could or should be resolved is not addressed; how to mediate them is left to the reader. Instead, the document simply asserts that they are "compatible with" the "consensus in the basic truths" it articulates.

Undoubtedly, all three texts have informed unfolding relations between different churches and communions and fostered a deepening of confidence in common action as described above. Yet there is also a residual sense of disappointment that they did not lead directly to the kind of breakthrough that might have been hoped for by those who produced them, and indeed by those who initially received them with great enthusiasm. Agreement on the doctrine of justification might have been expected to be a pivotal moment leading towards reconciliation between Lutherans and Catholics, given the acknowledgement on both sides that disagreement on this doctrine was the cardinal issue in Luther's break with papal authority and establishment of churches outside communion with continuing Catholicism. Yet it has not precipitated an expression of communion in common action that is different in kind from what there had been before, or that would be newly visible to the world beyond the Church.

Baptism, Eucharist and Ministry has influenced many initiatives towards greater unity, including those in which Anglican churches have participated, not least the Porvoo Agreement. Yet in some respects the convergence has weakened since the 1980s—for instance, in relation to baptism as sacramental initiation. Again, by and large, churches that were separated then remain separated now.

The reception of the *Final Report* proceeded differently in both communions, being swifter and more straightforward in coming to a positive conclusion in the Anglican Communion. Even there, agreement on the first two statements (on Eucharist and on ministry and ordination) was not matched by the level of agreement on the second two (on authority in the Church, which struggled with the Church of England's break from communion with churches under the primacy of the Bishop of Rome in the 16th century. Moreover, intensifying disagreement on what might be considered the lesser matter of the ordination of women contributed to the failure of ARCIC's work to open immediately visible doors in the practical expression of ecclesial communion through common action, including eucharistic sharing. Continuing disagreement made it more difficult to imagine what full reconciliation between the two communions might actually mean.[17] With the prospect of such reconciliation receding, it also became harder to situate the agreed statements of the first round of ARCIC as points on a journey toward a destination of full communion that might be reached in the lifetime of current participants in ecumenical work. Without that sense of momentum and accompanying hope for unity, what purchase can such agreements have? Likewise, some might ask: what harm can continuing disagreements really do?

---

17 Jeremy Worthen, "Ecumenical Dialogue and the Question of Authority" in *Incarnating Authority: A Critical Account of Authority in the Church*, ed. Paul Avis, Angela Berlis, Nikolaus Knoepffler, Martin O'Malley (München: Utzverlag, 2019), 191–208.

(3) AGREEMENT THAT BECOMES POSSIBLE BECAUSE OF COMMUNION, DISAGREEMENT THAT PREVENTS THIS

Agreement is an action that follows from the relationship of communion as well as an action that articulates it and enables its expression in practice. Because we are in communion, that is, we have Christ in common, we are able to speak and act together in the name of Christ. Any degree of communion between churches must open this possibility, while the term *full communion* implies that faith and order are as fully shared as can be conceived, short of merger. Yet ecumenical relationships of inter-ecclesial communion have struggled at this point.

As an illustration, one might consider the Leuenberg Agreement and the Community of Protestant Churches in Europe (CPCE) founded from it, now encompassing most of the historic Protestant churches across the European Continent and extending to the British Isles. Originally focused on "pulpit and table fellowship," the language of communion has increasingly come to the fore to describe the relation between the member churches.[18] What possibilities does this communion create, however, for agreeing to common action? Such agreement in the case of social bodies hinges on the exercise of authority. Authority enables a social actor to make a commitment or promise to bind the institution and its members to a particular course

---

18 See the document of the 2018 CPCE Assembly, "Church Communion," available online.

of action, position, or set of principles.[19] Without authority, binding agreement is not possible for social actors; promising is not possible. A group of representative persons, duly appointed, may agree among themselves, but this cannot be interpreted to mean that the church they represent has agreed to this position or action. Insofar as the member churches of CPCE remain wholly autonomous and do not accord ecclesial authority to its governance, the communion they share does not make possible actions of agreement that could be understood as commitments on the part of the churches that share in that communion.

At this point, we need to come back to the historic entangling of the Anglican Communion's self-understanding with its engagement in the ecumenical movement. The insistence on the fourth element of the Chicago-Lambeth Quadrilateral, the historic episcopate, which has been so perplexing to many ecumenists from Protestant churches, could be read as registering that union of churches and communion between churches both require common acceptance of a certain kind of ecclesial authority, namely, the authority that has been carried by those who share in the "historic episcopate." Yet from the time the Quadrilateral was drafted, Anglicans have carried a deep-seated ambivalence as to what kind of authority bishops in the historic episcopate may exercise beyond the province in which their see is located. The influence of the conciliar tradition on Anglicanism may be profound, but Anglicans have been wary of ascribing binding as opposed

19   David J. Stagaman, *Authority in the Church* (Collegeville, Minnesota: Liturgical Press, 1999).

to advisory authority to any "council" of the Communion as such.[20]

The role of the Lambeth Conference has been delicately poised here. Despite periodic discussions, its authority has been carefully limited to something *other* than a formal synod or council. Yet, as a gathering of all bishops of the Communion, it creates the possibility of those bishops agreeing to an action or position that they will each take back and commend with the authority they have in their diocese and Province as actions or positions shared by all who belong within the historic episcopate of the Anglican Communion. According to the 1930 Lambeth Conference, the churches of the Communion "are bound together not by a central legislative and executive authority, but by mutual loyalty sustained through the common counsel of the bishops in conference."[21] The 1948 Conference made it clearer still that the absence of "a central legislative and executive authority" did not mean there was no authority in the Communion. Rather, "the positive nature of the authority which binds the Anglican Communion together is therefore seen to be moral and spiritual, resting on the truth of the Gospel, and on a charity which is patient and willing to defer to the common mind."[22]

Something similar, if also different, might be said about the other three instruments of communion. In each case, they open up a space for

---

20 See R. William Franklin, "Conciliarism and the Ecclesiology of The Episcopal Church: A Review of Resources on the Authority of the General Convention," *Sewanee Theological Review*, 61/2 (2018): 447–94.

21 Lambeth Conference 1930, Resolution 49(c), available online.

22 Committee Report on "The Anglican Communion" in *The Lambeth Conference 1948: The Encyclical Letter from the Bishops; Together with Resolutions and Reports* (London: SPCK, 1948), II.84.

actions of agreement that, while not legally binding, carry a potential weight of authority, not least with regard to communication with ecumenical partners. For instance, the Anglican Consultative Council, meeting in 2016, passed a resolution regarding the *Joint Declaration on the Doctrine of Justification*. The Lambeth Conference of 1988 responded to ARCIC I's *Final Report* and to *Baptism, Eucharist and Ministry*.[23] The challenges, however, of discerning and deferring to "the common mind" of the Communion, with "mutual loyalty sustained through the common counsel of the bishops in conference," have become especially acute since the turn of the millennium.

It is noteworthy in this context that, in practice, Anglican churches also seem to have accepted that relations of "full communion" with other, non-Anglican churches will mean weaker authority for common commitments than that which exists between the churches of the Anglican Communion. This is true even where the churches involved are located in the same place and country and might be expected to benefit from the capacity to make such commitments together. In the post-war decades, Lambeth Conferences gave encouragement to the idea of a "Wider Episcopal Fellowship" that would gather all bishops who were in communion with bishops of the Anglican Communion, including those from the Old Catholic Churches of the Union of Utrecht and the Church of South India, as an extension of the Lambeth Conference.[24] Ultimately, it never quite materialised and was quietly abandoned. The assumption behind it, however—that

---

23 Anglican Consultative Council 16, Resolution 16; Lambeth Conference 1988, Resolution 8: both available online.

24 See, e.g., Lambeth Conference 1958, Resolution 16, available online.

where churches are in communion, the bishops who oversee that relation of communion should gather periodically for counsel and to seek agreement where appropriate—seems entirely right. Why would Anglicans insist on the historic episcopate for communion between churches unless bishops have a distinctive role not just in articulating such communion but in enlivening it and enabling it to realise its creative possibilities?

One reason, among many, why this has proved difficult in practice is the lack of agreement on the nature and exercise of episcopal authority. While there are some significant variations here within the Anglican Communion, they extend further in the case of the churches with which particular Anglican churches are in communion, like Lutheran and Moravian churches. The importance of clergy and laity being represented alongside bishops in the councils of the church has also come more to the fore over the past hundred years, for Anglicans as well as others, making gatherings of bishops alone look somewhat anomalous as a focus for authority. Moreover, while formal agreements for communion with other churches often include a commitment to consultation, that does not necessarily lead to a capacity to come to agreements that the churches will recognise as their own; nor does it lead to what *The Church: Towards a Common Vision* described as communion "in structures of conciliar relations and decision-making" as a necessary element of "full communion."[25] While inter-ecclesial communion brings the possibility of making agreements that express the common life of the churches in new ways, therefore, for various reasons it has proved resistant to realization.

---

25   WCC Commission on Faith and Order, *The Church*, §37.

PROSPECTIVE MEASURES

In each of the three types of relation between communion, agreement, and disagreement, disagreement marks the limit of attempts to articulate, express, and enact agreement between churches corresponding to the degree of communion they share. In the first case, agreement that articulates communion: disagreement as a failure to agree together in our ecclesial actions following from the faith we share places a question mark against the kind of relation we actually have to one another. In the second case, agreement that enables the expression of the gift of communion in common action: continuing disagreements serve as one of the causes that prevent churches acting on the imperative to grow into the fullness of the common life that they see themselves sharing. In the third case, agreement that becomes possible because of the relation of communion: disagreements about oversight and authority may play a significant role in frustrating this; likewise a lack of clarity about what it means to be in communion with one another through Christ, and specifically what is expected with regard to acting and speaking as one.

The foregoing analysis suggests that critical to addressing disagreements in ecumenical contexts may be seeking consensus about the kind of agreements that properly correspond to being in (full) communion with one another. Likewise, mutual understanding should be achieved about the ways in which such agreements may be articulated in the different ecclesiological languages of the participating churches, such that what one offers can be received by others. Without some clarity on these two questions, it is bound to be difficult to enact with confidence ecclesial agreements that articulate and affirm communion between churches; to build on that with agreements that enable common action expressing that communion; and to find ways to make new agreements together that convey authoritative commitments in mission. That would seem to be at least part of the explanation as to why so many formal ecumenical agreements of various kinds over the last five decades have failed to inaugurate transforming change in the way our churches live out their communion with one another in Christ. Duly marking the difficulty of securing agreement between churches with differing ecclesiologies may help us to see not only the limiting aspects of our disagreements but also, by dint of recognition, their potential for drawing us into deeper understanding, hence more complete agreement and fuller communion. Critical, too, will be a *desire* for visible unity, which, the ecumenical movement has always said, is a spiritual matter, planted by God in the hearts of individual believers through prayer.

FIVE

Ecclesiology & Conflict

Ecumenical and Interreligious Perspectives

Margaret R. Rose

Given the global tensions so evident in our [Communion] today, we do not accept that there is any one issue of difference or contention which can, or indeed would ever cause us to break our unity as represented by our common baptism. Neither would we consider severing the deep and abiding bonds of affection which characterize our relationships as Anglican women.... This sisterhood of suffering is at the heart of our theology and our commitment to transforming the world through peace with justice. Rebuilding and reconciling the world are central to our faith.[1]

---

1 "Women's Statement" by Anglican and Episcopal delegates to the United Nations Commission on the Status of Women (New York, March 2007), available online at anglicannews.org.

Every year since 1947, the United Nations Commission on the Status of Women welcomes representatives from around the world: delegates from member states, NGOs, and numerous ecumenical and other faith-based organizations. Starting in 1995, small delegations of two or three Anglican women participated. But in 2007, thanks to the work of the Anglican Communion Office and the Women's Ministries Office of the Episcopal Church, primates from 34 provinces sent a delegation of 50 women and 10 girls to represent female Anglicans at the annual meeting. Accompanied and hosted by Ecumenical Women 2000, Anglican women worked, worshipped, and advocated alongside Christians and other people of faith from around the world. That year, the Anglican delegation was the largest among the faith bodies, and its members made their voices heard, speaking out about the Beijing Platform for Action as well as a lack of representation, both in their respective countries and in their beloved churches.

Then as now, the unity of the Anglican Communion was threatened by disagreements, not least on issues related to sexuality. The women at UNCSW, however, were not deterred from working together to help eradicate poverty and hunger, end rape as a weapon of war, combat trafficking, and promote equal education, amid much else. Speaking out loud and in public as women impelled by faith, they felt they could make a difference, not only in the world but also in the Church. At the close of the 2007 meeting, the delegation issued a unanimous "Word," sent to the Archbishop of Canterbury and all the primates of the Communion, which called on these leaders to recognize suffering as a primary bond.[2] Empowered by their connection in the Anglican Communion and in solidarity with women from around the world, they laid claim to their unity—not of doctrine, in the first place, but of commitment to a better world for themselves and their children.

The women spoke not from positions of power but as a group linked by their experience. Formed variously as members of the Mother's Union and of altar guilds, as parish workers and advocates, as deacons and priests, they were strengthened not only by their connection as Anglicans but also by the diverse context of the United Nations and the many faith-filled voices whose work had a common goal. Their call to unity, formulated at a time of inter-Anglican conflict, was based on the bond of baptism, on bonds of affection, and on a kind of suffering that understood its source of strength as rooted in the very suffering of Jesus.

Recounting this story tells you something about my perspective on the questions at hand. I approach the themes of communion and disagreement, ecclesiology and conflict, from the experiences, methods, and insights of ecumenical and interreligious work. My experience as parish priest, rector, community organizer, feminist, and child of the U.S. South informs and shapes a commitment and passion for justice, reconciliation, and unity. My current work as the Presiding Bishop's Deputy for Ecumenical and Interreligious Relations places

2 See *Anglican Women on Church and Mission*, ed. Berling, Kwok, and TePaa (Harrisburg: Morehouse Publishing, 2013). Cf. resolution 31 submitted to the 13th meeting of the Anglican Consultative Council in Nottingham, 2005, available online.

equal emphasis on each part. Both aspects of the work are concerned to create spaces in which we can actively learn from one another instead of acquiescing to separate silos, even when our long-term goals may be different.

PAYING ATTENTION TO THE WORLD

From a Christian-ecclesial perspective, ecumenical and interreligious work is essentially diaconal. It is service for the Church and for the sake of the gospel, just as the liturgy of Ordination of a Deacon suggests: "to interpret to the Church the needs, concerns, and hopes of the world."[3] Doing this work well requires directing attention outside church structures, paying heed to precisely *the world*—globally and locally, politically and socially. This work requires us to link arms lovingly with partners who are Christian, "interfaith," or otherwise unaffiliated. In doing so, we shape our own prayer (and liturgy), social action, community life, and sharing of the gospel. Engaging the world from the margins, from the outside in, allows the Church to ask about others' needs and build a capacity to respond. As with the Anglican women at the United Nations, the diverse contexts of ecumenical and interreligious work both confirm and strengthen identity and open new ways of seeing and understanding our efforts toward unity.

Several instances of recent projects in our Ecumenical and Interreligious Office may help to illustrate the proper breadth of this work.

---

3   The Book of Common Prayer (1979), 543.

In the fall of 2019, the World Council of Churches hosted its first Interfaith Officers gathering in Cardiff, Wales, where Christian partners shared perspectives and action plans from various contexts around the world. Participants included Bishop Joseph Wandera from Kenya, as well as interfaith officers from India, Malaysia, Pakistan, South Africa, several countries in Europe, Canada, and the United States. Each spoke of the increasing connections between ecumenical and interreligious work, most particularly where so-called religious violence and bias are becoming an ever more present reality.

In December 2019, the 6th Annual Assembly of the Forum for Promoting Peace in Muslim Communities took place in Abu Dhabi and concluded with the signing of a Charter of New Alliance of Virtues. The forum, hosted by Muslim leaders with guests from Jewish and Christian traditions, was notable for the diversity of participants and the range of political and theological viewpoints. The presence of American evangelicals, in particular, underscored the changing and broader landscape of inter-religious engagement. It also provided, in this Muslim-hosted space, opportunity for conversations among Christians who are not so accustomed to speaking on our home turf.[4]

In the United States, the Episcopal Church, like many of our partners, conducts much of its interreligious work through the National Council of Churches of Christ in the USA (NCC). The Jewish-Christian dialogue, co-led by the National Council of Synagogues and the NCC, met recently in Pittsburgh. On the agenda was a visit to the Tree of Life Synagogue, where 11 worshippers were killed in 2018 by a

---

4   See Peter Welby, "An alliance of people of goodwill," available online at arabnews.com.

shooter shouting anti-Jewish epithets. As Jewish partners shared with us the experience of witnessing that event, they helped us understand how Christians and others could join in solidarity to address increased anti-Semitism and anti-Jewish bias in the U.S. and beyond.

The Episcopal Church also participates in official bilateral ecumenical dialogues with a view to reconciliation. For instance, the Anglican–Roman Catholic Consultation in the U.S. has taken up race as the focus of its current round, in a paper that jumps off from critical reflections on our political and historical context before turning to Scripture and sacraments in a mode of lament *and* hope. Meanwhile, the Evangelical Lutheran Church in America has initiated a conversation with several, predominantly white, mainline churches to address issues of white supremacy in the United States; and other such fora are emerging, as well, in a bid to work across theological, social, and political divides of our time. All of these have been and will continue to be challenging conversations, as they seek and expose the foundations and sources of our current division. In every case, participants articulate a clear yearning for reconciliation, starting with respect for differences of perspective.

No such meeting was more significant than the October 2019 Christian Unity Gathering of the NCC, during which participants made a pilgrimage to the sight of the first landing of Africans in 1619 at Pt. Comfort in Hampton, Virginia. We now recognize how thoroughly the prosperity of the United States—and that of many of its churches—rests upon indelible features of our colonial past: the stealing of land from indigenous peoples and theft of the labor of enslaved others. Any conversation about Christian unity in the United States must take into consideration the weight of these foundational realities. Truth-telling about historical beginnings and engaging a process of recognition, repentance, and reconciliation among the churches are commitments that offer new perspectives on the work toward Christian unity. Speaking in 1963, Martin Luther King noted that "11 AM on Sunday morning is the most segregated hour in America." Alas, for Christians in the U.S. who still attend church, this largely remains true.

REVEALING UNITY

If ecumenical pedagogy is, for Christians, a diaconal activity of "paying attention and telling," the ecumenical task may be summed up in the ancient words now embedded in Eucharistic Prayer D of the 1979 BCP, where we place the Church before God, asking him to "reveal its unity, guard its faith, and preserve it in peace."[5] The Church mentioned here is neither the Episcopal Church nor the Anglican Communion alone. With all Christians and churches, across time and space, the liturgy bids us identify, treasure, and protect those common goods that perdure: above all, the holy scriptures, and also the struggles of the earliest churches, countless missionary ventures, and thousands of synods and councils. Among these last, we recall the Council of Jerusalem as described in Acts 15, which wrestled its way both to blessing diversity and articulating boundaries for membership in Christian communities. As ever, our call to unity is not to a

---

5   BCP 1979, 375.

distant, idealized past but rather to fresh reception of the one revelation we have had all along, which speaks again and again.

To be sure, the current social and political context in the United States (as in other places) hinders our obedience, blinding us to creative ways forward. Political and social polarization, autocratic leaders, and lack of civil and civic discourse form a backdrop to the reality of declining church affiliation and attendant anxiety. Sad to say, an atmosphere of fear creates a culture of inwardness—battening down the hatches and clinging to past ways of thinking and acting, rather than fostering openness to new ideas, engagement with others, and attention to the *unity* that amazingly perdures. Amid this disorder, we should hope to hear a new word in the increasing awareness that what separates us is not simply diversity or disagreement—which may actually enhance unity—but the pervasive effects of racism and colonialism woven into American society. As we attend to the contextual specificity of our lives and churches, we may be able to see some of the sources of our blindness.

We find such a recognition in the 2018 Episcopal–United Methodist proposal for full communion, *A Gift to the World: Co-Laborers for the Healing of Brokenness.* The dialogue, which began in 2002, grew increasingly aware of the need to address issues of race and class in addition to doctrine. The proposal cites theological and historical work on the understanding of *episcopé*, the contours of the Chicago-Lambeth Quadrilateral, and goals for joint mission and ministry. But its principal contribution is the recognition that, despite the shared history of our churches, racism has played and continues to play a crucial role in division between them. The proposal's "gift to the world" is thus commitment to the work of anti-racism. As the authors recount:

In addition to our common forebears John and Charles Wesley, we also have common forebears in Richard Allen and Absalom Jones, both members of St. George's Methodist Episcopal Church in Philadelphia. Due to policies of racial exclusion, Richard Allen would go on to found what would become the African Methodist Episcopal Church, while Absalom Jones would become the first African American priest ordained in The Episcopal Church. We recognize the lasting sin of racism in our society and our churches, and affirm the need for ongoing repentance, truth telling, and work for racial justice and healing.[6]

Addressing these issues in ecumenical dialogues marks a small but critical step in recognizing both injustices of society and the causes of division.

The way forward, or the way to be revealed, will not *begin* with full visible unity or agreement in doctrine, though it may end there. Instead, we can take heart from the new beginning of Pentecost described in Acts 2: people from every "tribe, language, people and nation" hearing and understanding in their own native tongue. Acts 2 reverses Babel not as a return to one language, but by modeling many ways of speaking in which each is understood. The challenge and opportunity of this vision for a globalized world is immense. In his commentary on Acts, Willie James Jennings describes our pentecostal work as requiring "bodies that reach across massive and real boundaries,

---

6   *A Gift to the World: Co-Laborers for the Healing of Brokenness*, being a proposal for full communion by the Episcopal Church and the United Methodist Church (2018), available online.

cultural, religious, and ethnic."[7] "What God had always spoken to Israel," Jennings observes, "God now speaks even more loudly in the voices of the many to the many."[8]

Pentecost enacts, over and over, an uncomfortable diversity. God's divinely designed unity requires listening to a multitude of voices, including those that have yet to speak. In our western and mainline context, we should hope to hear from those known as Nones, those who identify as SBR (spiritual but not religious), Multiple Belongers (who identify with several traditions), and certainly members of new Pentecostal and Evangelical Churches who have not previously engaged formal ecumenical work but are among the fastest growing groups of Christians within the vast and expansive household of God.

In this evolving western context, the distinction between Life and Work on the one hand and Faith and Order on the other requires reframing. The World Council of Churches' landmark document on ecclesiology, *Baptism, Eucharist and Ministry (1982),* powerfully articulated grounds for a broad sacramental convergence and consensus. This foundational work has helped all the churches advance not only in mutual recognition of one another, but also in common mission. The WCC's more recent *Church: Toward a Common Vision* (2015) effectively addresses the emerging social issues in the life of the world and the Church and notes the moral and ethical challenges posed by differing interpretations of the gospel. The document invites

---

7   Willie James Jennings, *Acts: A Theological Commentary on the Bible* (Louisville, KY: John Knox Press, 2017), 32.

8   *Ibid.*

the churches to discern together those issues—including matters of sexuality, marriage, reproductive rights, migration, poverty, and race—that are "church dividing."

Since the World Council's Busan Assembly of 2009, Faith and Order discussion has probed more deeply into these moral and ethical questions, taking time to set them within a larger social analysis. The WCC has also been transformed by the extraordinary growth of churches in the Global South, which are now helping to shape the conversation. Professor Ellen Wondra, an Episcopal Church member of the Commission, notes that "gender, race/ethnicity, colonialism, and migration are properly theological and moral issues" that fall within the purview of Faith and Order. Likewise, a shift away from the agenda of "the North" to the concerns of the Global South, she says, has led to greater emphasis on moral questions concerning the economy, poverty, migration, use of resources, and the environment.[9] In this way, *life and faith, work and order* all together help us to listen across difference and celebrate the gifts such listening brings.

RECEPTIVE ECUMENISM, EXCHANGE OF GIFTS

The movement of receptive ecumenism, focused on the "exchange of gifts" between partners, has proved essential in this work.[10] Rather

---

9   Ellen Wondra, private communication, December 18, 2019.

10   *Receptive Ecumenism and the Call to Catholic Learning*, ed. Paul D. Murray (New York: Oxford University Press, 2008).

than attempting to convince or teach the other about the rightness of one's own way, we strive to listen for what we can learn. Might unity, or the beginnings of reconciliation, be found in seeking out and listening for the differences we take to divide us?

The work of anti-racism proves instructive here. Often, trainings seek what different racial groups have in common, with the tacit assumption that "All are alike under the skin" or "All want the same things." This may not be the case. Recent work in this area demonstrates that ways of sharing, distributing, seeking justice, and proclaiming the realm of God are not identical. The differences are significant and valuable.

Similarly, ecumenical dialogues have often focused on commonalities, attempting to find enough shared doctrinal ground for a full communion agreement. In the case of interreligious dialogue, we have proposed that "the same God loves and creates all" or "all religions are peace-loving" or "all accept the Golden Rule." While there may be truth in such claims, these dialogues have often functioned more as self-projection than as occasions for knowing, engaging, and appreciating the gifts and perspectives of others. Truly getting to know others who are *not like us* helps us encounter others and recognize our own shortcomings and sins. How might naming the gifts of difference be transformative for all? What would discussions of unity yield if they began with the question, "What voices are not at the table?"

Amid these realities, interreligious engagement and dialogue offer yet another look. The so-called religious other, those most far away in faith and doctrine, surely invite us to new ways of seeing and hearing. From these engagements, we learn better to understand and respond to the call of unity in diversity.

An invitation to this work may be found in *Engaging Others, Knowing Ourselves,* published by the Evangelical Lutheran Church in America, a full-communion partner of the Episcopal Church for more than 20 years. This resource, drawn from the experience of diverse communities throughout the U.S., was developed as the ELCA looked forward to its inter-religious policy statement.[11] The book's title promises what the collected case studies demonstrate, namely, that engaging religious "others" does not erase our commitments and identity but, on the contrary, strengthen them. As we, in turn, offer insights, practices, gifts, and our own shortcomings, we come to know ourselves more deeply even as we grow in appreciation of the religious diversity of the communities in which we live. In this way, resources developed for interreligious relations offer tools for ecumenical work as well.

What are the practical applications of moving away from sameness while working together for a common future? In these divided times, how are bridges built, while appreciating difference and recognizing that some divisions cannot be ignored because they come from injustice and sin that continue to cause suffering? As Margaret O'Gara suggests in her book *Ecumenical Gift Exchange,* listening for and receiving the gifts of the other is a work of the Holy Spirit, as denominations discover more of what binds them together, even as they

---

11   See *Engaging Others Knowing Ourselves: A Lutheran Calling in an Inter-Religious World*, ed. Carol Schersten LaHurd, Darrell Jodock, and Kathryn Lohre (Minneapolis: Lutheran University Press, 2016). Cf. the ELCA's Inter-Religious Policy Statement, "A Declaration of Inter-Religious Commitment," available online.

seriously discuss and assess crucial differences.[12]

How could this pedagogy of deep listening be used not only in ecumenical and interreligious conversation, but also in intra-church conversation, that is, among partners seeking to be and/or remain in communion?

WAY OF LOVE, CARE FOR THE POOR, SISTERHOOD OF SUFFERING

The Episcopal Church is not alone in facing the challenges of continuing communion within its worldwide body. The recent struggles of the United Methodist Church, the membership of which spans the globe, are at least analogous. Just here, the 2019 text, *Sent in Love: A United Methodist Understanding of the Church,* helpfully resources the necessary work of seeking deeper unity amid difference, sans uniformity. As is increasingly common, intra-denominational contestation inspires a rearticulation of basic ecumenical principles. In the words of *Sent in Love:*

> Together with other Christians, United Methodists declare the essential oneness of the Church in Christ Jesus even as we lament the sinful divisions which continue to mark its pilgrimage through history. Trusting in the community-creating power of God's love, United Methodists have expressed a commitment to overcome

---

12 Margaret O'Gara, *The Ecumenical Gift Exchange* (Collegeville: Liturgical Press, 1998).

these divisions—both within our own denominations and the church universal....

We are brought together by grace, not because we share the same views, customs, cultural practice or even moral convictions. When such differences are held in the midst of a deeper and richer unity, they do not threaten the fellowship God intends, but instead enhance it.[13]

To be sure, none of us possess a governance outline or structure for navigating "when churches in communion disagree." We are all trying to learn to live in patience and charity with multiple theological and ecclesiological conflicts, and a breadth of strongly held convictions. Nevertheless, if race, poverty, migration, gender, and sexuality also divide us, to one degree and another, might other factors and powers help provide unity? Duly noting the explosiveness of some social issues, we should and can claim anew the power of Christ-formed love, in which the sisterhood and brotherhood of suffering may properly be formed, in solidarity with the poor.

St. Paul sets a good example. While we find in Acts a model of unity in diversity (ch. 2) and the inauguration of conciliar decision making (ch. 15), we find in Paul's teaching about justification a conviction that all are children of God through faith (see Gal. 2:15-20; 3:26-29). Importantly, this teaching follows from Paul's acceptance of a kind of unity in diversity, according to which the faithful children of God may pursue distinct but complementary ministries. As

---

13 *Sent in Love: A United Methodist Understanding of the Church*, §§101, 108, available online.

Paul writes:

> When James and Cephas and John, who were acknowledged pillars, recognized the grace that had been given to me, they gave to Barnabas and me the right hand of fellowship, agreeing that we should go to the Gentiles and they to the circumcised. They asked only one thing, that we remember the poor, which was actually what I was eager to do. (Gal. 2:9-10)

That Paul and Cephas could arrive at such a peace is instructive, given their enduring differences of opinion. Focused together on the poor, they apparently agreed to disagree about how the acts of the Council of Jerusalem ought to apply in one and another place.

Since his 2015 election as Presiding Bishop of the Episcopal Church, Michael Curry has urged a *way of love* as the ground for unity—for Episcopalians, for Anglicans, and as a Christian offering to the world. With reference to the Anglican Communion, Bishop Curry has spoken of the remarkable Primates' Meeting of January 2016, Archbishop Welby's first, at which the points of disagreement about sexuality were discussed openly and charitably, and all agreed to try to walk together. "What we didn't know was whether you could hold together with this much profound diversity and disagreement," recalls Curry. For his part, he spoke to his fellow primates (a majority of whom are African) as "a descendent, a child of the African diaspora," but more especially

> because we are all related: We are brothers and sisters in Jesus Christ, and he taught us to love each other. ... You are my brothers

and I love you and we will walk this journey together. We have done what we have done in our [Episcopal] church because we believe everybody is a child of God, no matter your sexual orientation, or your sexuality, or your gender identity, or your race, or your politics. Everybody is made in the image of God. We believe this is love's way.... That same love for our brothers and sisters who are gay and lesbian, bisexual, transgender is the same love I have for you.[14]

This Way of Love has become a central focus of Bishop Curry's tenure as Presiding Bishop. The website of the Episcopal Church describes it as a "rule of life, as old as the church itself."[15] We walk this way, in part, by *turning* to follow Jesus, which the New Testament calls *metanoia*. To quote the website again: "With God's help we can turn from the powers of sin, hatred, fear, injustice, and oppression toward the way of truth, love, hope, justice, and freedom. In turning, we reorient our lives to Jesus Christ, falling in love again, again, and again."[16] Cannot this turning describe, as well, a new way of life in the Church? Can we not commit to new ways of engaging and loving one another, new ways of looking to Christ and experiencing unity?

While loving God and neighbor, serving the poor, and persevering in a solidarity of suffering do not produce a plan for the Church's governance, nor erase our social, cultural, and theological differences,

---

14 Goldman Sachs, "Talks at GS: The Most Rev. Michael Curry, Presiding Bishop of The Episcopal Church," available online at youtube.com.

15 See "The Way of Love" on the website of the Episcopal Church, at episcopalchurch.org/way-of-love.

16 See "Turn," at episcopalchurch.org/way-of-love/practice/turn.

they do provide a point of orientation and departure from which to do the work. As the Anglican women at the U.N. proudly proclaimed, our sisterhood (and brotherhood) of suffering love, in Christ and his baptism, will show us the way in which we must walk.

SIX

Seeds of Reconciliation in Kenya

Joseph Wandera

INTRODUCTION

God's mission of reconciliation and the proclamation of good news to all people is the mandate of the Church in all ages. In the all-too-common context of suspicion and conflict in and between Christian communities, God's invitation to reconciliation becomes even more urgent.

Inter-communal conversation fulfils an important aspect of resolution I.10 of Lambeth Conference 1998, which urged Anglicans to listen to one another and foster resources for understanding and working together in spite of our differences, so as to seek the mind of Christ. Today, we find ourselves immersed in even more relationships in our globalized world. Yet over the past 14 years the Anglican Communion has modeled probably the most visible front of Church disunity, tearing the Communion apart in significant ways. Bishops around the world, not least in Nigeria, Uganda, and Kenya, have been vociferous in their condemnation of decisions taken by others regarding persons in same-sex relationships, and sometimes have threatened to delink from the Anglican Communion. Such critical voices surmise that our brothers and sisters in the northern hemisphere do not care what the rest of the Communion thinks about what they do. They argue that what is at play is not just a crisis of faith but also a crisis of selfishness.

At a recent meeting of the House of Bishops in the Anglican Church of Kenya, the question of our participation in the forthcoming Lambeth Conference was discussed at length. A handful of bishops argued that they would not attend the meeting because the Archbishop of Canterbury had invited bishops in practicing same-sex relations to be in attendance against the spirit of Lambeth 1998 I.10. Others, however, took a more conciliatory tone, seeing God's call to fellowship as superseding current disagreements and calling for efforts toward restoration of relationships. Sadly, the objections by the first group of bishops has been loud enough to suppress other voices, in Kenya and in the broader African context.

There is plenty dysfunction here to go around. The presentation of "the south" as always being united in one perspective and one voice is a construction of westerners who want to enlist an imagined unified authoritarian Southern Voice in our battles over human sexuality. At the same time, leaders in Africa are often too happy to overlook their own differences, if only it can bring them a certain leverage or voice in the global arena of church debates. And, of course, in other parts of Africa, churches have been more tolerant of diverse views—as in the Anglican Church in Southern Africa, for instance, which allows individual provinces to make their own decisions on the question.

The following paper records various voices of Kenyan bishops, showing that they are far from unanimous in their approach to this question. In fact, they articulate a number of perspectives, some of which invite opportunities for reconciliation in the Anglican family and offer a glimpse into what churches in communion may do when they disagree. In this way, the Kenyan bishops collectively help us imagine constructive engagement in the Communion.

ANGLICAN AGONIES IN KENYAN PERSPECTIVE

A few brief historical notes will help us locate present-day discussions among Kenyan Anglicans.

The Anglican Church of Kenya was founded by the Church Missionary Society (CMS) and is the oldest and largest Protestant church in Kenya with a membership of over five million. The first CMS missionary, Dr. Johann Kraft, arrived in Mombasa in 1888. The movement in England was part of "a pan-European eighteenth-century Protestant revival of piety."[1] These evangelicals emphasized the im-

---

1   Rowan Strong, *Anglicanism and the British Empire, c.1700-1850* (Oxford: Oxford University Press, 2007), 11-12.

portance of individual encounter with the divine, culminating in conversion. In Africa, the conversion motif was unmistakable. According to E. S. Atieno Odhiambo, citing Max Warren, the four priorities of evangelicals were proclaiming the "word of God" in a sinful world, conversion, trusting the Holy Spirit's refashioning of a new man, and the priesthood of all believers. On all counts, every practicing Christian was encouraged to distinguish good from evil, the convert from the non-convert, and the pagan from the Christian.[2]

In turn, the advent of the East African Revival Movement in the late 1920s and 1930s shaped the theological thinking and practices of most Anglican leaders. The movement of the *Balokole* (saved ones) emphasized personal renewal, public confession and salvation, and fellowship. A binary evangelical outlook came to characterize Christian theology and practice in East Africa in a profound way. This heritage has influenced present positions on matters affecting the Anglican Communion and attendant contestations in Kenya and elsewhere.

Religion has often been studied as a system of symbols that exist independent of actors.[3] However, more recent scholars of religion have paid attention to individuals and, significantly, to the dialectical relationship between systems and actors. In this approach, a focus on individual religious leaders may yield insight into the relationship between religious discourses and broader communal dynamics. As

2 E. S. Atieno Odhiambo, *The Paradox of Collaboration and Other Essays* (Nairobi: East African Literature Bureau, 1974), 104.

3 See Clifford Geertz, *Interpretation of Culture* (New York: Basic Books, 1973), 470-473.

artifacts of a political culture, the respective discourses reveal prevalent public opinion on issues that directly or indirectly affect members of society.

This analytical premise assumes that the way individuals speak can create and recreate a positive or negative social reality within which to view others. In other words, the construction of society provides for the articulation of differences, rendered as generalized meanings though only within specific symbol systems. In that sense, discourse (language) is a form of social praxis and a source of social transformation. The critical discourse perspective provides a framework within which to address the cultural-linguistic ideas and practices that generate disharmony.

Contestation in the Anglican Communion has a long history. However, the immediate background is the 1998 Lambeth Conference and resolution I.10, which viewed same-sex activity as sinful, and something from which to repent and change direction. Successive primates' meetings upheld the resolution as the standard of Anglican teaching on sexuality. African discussions of same-sex relations have, moreover, often centered on its alleged nonbiblical basis, on a wider growth of secularism, and the problem of western individualism.

By all accounts, developments in two dioceses, aided by their provinces, sped along the present crisis. The Diocese of New Hampshire in the United States elected Gene Robinson, a divorced person and practicing homosexual. In turn, the General Convention of the Episcopal Church confirmed the election, and Presiding Bishop Frank Griswold served as chief consecrator, over the objections of his fellow primates. In Canada, the Diocese of New Westminster approved public rites for the blessing of same-sex unions. In turn, the General Synod of the Anglican Church of Canada affirmed the "integrity and sanctity" of same-sex relationships. The Lambeth Commission's *Windsor Report* (2004) responded in real time to these developments, calling for restraint, further study, and structural reforms in aid of common decision-making, not least to counter cross-border interventions that introduced further instability.

In Kenya, these developments produced both shock and anxiety, and generated considerable conversation. Here, I wish to turn especially to a contextual analysis of intra-Kenyan discourse. Again, contextualizing any debate enables an appreciation of the authenticity and uniqueness of varying experiences. It also usefully lodges a protest against the tendency to impose a universal paradigm or totalizing agenda. Finally, contextualization *from below* helps us see how interactions are conceived and experienced indigenously.

We often assume that religious actors speak with one voice and in this way can help stem hostilities. The former assumption is not true, but the latter is: in Kenya, bishops preside over large areas and wield significant influence. By virtue of their positions, they can open doors for bridge building during times of suspicion and conflict. Their perspectives vary, however, and thus are "multi-vocal." Taken together, they might also be viewed as ambivalent, as one and another voice can be heard as exacerbating exclusion or jeopardizing cohesion, while others perhaps provide opportunities for concord. They all find a certain discursive home, however, within the context of contemporary contestation within the Anglican family.

WHAT ARE KENYAN BISHOPS SAYING?

While numerous studies have been conducted on Anglican debates around same-sex sexuality, little attention has been paid to episcopal discourse and its impact on the Communion, especially in Africa. In fact, I have found no study focused on the potential for building bridges in this regard, even as African Anglican churches serve as powerful public institutions, both at home and abroad. Just here, I hope that the following discourse analysis of the views of Kenyan Anglican bishops on the matter of human sexuality in the Anglican Communion may shed some light on the state of the debate and the potential for progress in overcoming present conflicts.

Speaking with a random sample of Kenyan Anglican bishops in late 2019, I asked each one simply to reflect on current disagreements in the Anglican Communion.[4] Of the more than 20 interviews conducted, I here summarize and analyze nine from diverse backgrounds. They do not represent the views of all Kenyan bishops but display a breadth of perspectives.

> *Bishop 1.* I think that GAFCON [the Global Fellowship of Confessing Anglicans] axis has become obsessed with the matter of sexuality.... Secondly, I think the Archbishop of Canterbury should try to steer the Communion toward the gospel rather than simply discussing the issue of sexuality.... No more resolutions on sexuality, please!

4   The interviews were conducted in Kenya by use of telephone between 1 November and 28 December 2019.

Bishop 2. The Anglican Communion will survive the wave of acrimony not through intimidation ... but through tolerance and a penetration of truth.

Bishop 3. I strongly believe in people talking and I think it is in the interest of God who created us. When we don't talk, the disagreement enlarges. And that is what the Anglican Communion has experienced. In 2006, I went to GAFCON in Jerusalem. The people who organized it were already on the judgement throne, saying *others are sinners, don't follow them*. If you read, John 10:11-16, Jesus says "I am the good shepherd, who lays down his life for his sheep." They hear his voice as he also listens to them. You can't hear the voice of an enemy. If we really believe in the Communion, we must listen. In 2006 at GAFCON, I didn't like what the Archbishop of Uganda was saying when he said "there is nothing good at the Lambeth Conference, they are fallen." If I am fallen and we are walking together with you, do you leave me fallen? Fellowship and listening to one another is the key thing. God never distinguishes unfairly (Exod. 30:15). That is why I am going to the Lambeth Conference. I strongly believe that I should not be on the judgment throne. If I can help someone know that this is sin, why not. Dialogue and fellowship must be our business.

Bishop 4. First we need dialogue. There will be no solution if people do not agree to come together and discuss. It will not do any good, if people choose not to talk. I know bishops who are against this very thing. But again, by quitting, it will be assumed that you are defeated. Let's persist with engagement.

Bishop 5. We remain Christians so there is need to forgive each other and reconcile. The major problem is when one person does not see his or her wrong, to be able to say: *brother, I see I went wrong here, forgive me.* The words of Isaiah remain true: "Let us come and reason together." Churches are holders of peace, so they must share and reason together. The problem is that there is nobody talking to each other. But also, others are not hearing.

Bishop 6. We need to retreat and listen in humility to each other with a view to reconciling. Looking at the Bible as the primary document, and at associated texts, let us reflect on the biblical principle of the oneness of the Church (Eph. 4:3ff.). We must seek a solution in terms of reconciliation and forgiveness. At the same time, we should recognize that our different views on sexuality are more than emotive opinions. Let us not trivialize our varying biblical views, downplaying them to mere difference.

Bishop 7. Leaders will understand that we are family and disagreements will always be there. Next, we should build bridges of understanding through listening with intent. We need rules, regulations, and norms that will protect the dignity, integrity, and unity of the Communion. We should try to understand why people hold varying opinions. Different matters are properly private and public, which means a line should be drawn so that private life does not hinder ministry. While marriage is a public sacrament, it is also a mystery of God and act of grace. At the individual level, it should not be subjected to public scrutiny but rather tended to pastorally in love. Let us appreciate the things that unite us over against the things that divide. The Communion should enhance our linkages between churches through networking, visits and friendship, exchange programs, all of which will affirm our sense of belonging and celebrate our diversity of ministerial contexts.

Bishop 8. The straw that broke the camel's back was when churches accepted the homosexual agenda. We tried our best to defend our faith as given to us: that is why the Anglican Church was formed. In Canterbury in 1998, 70 Bishops voted in favour of homosexuality and 526 against (with 45 abstentions). When the Americans went back home, they consecrated Gene Robinson as bishop, who later divorced his partner. Our friends in the USA were being persecuted. When I raised my voice, they cut financial support. I looked for evangelical friends, a faith I could defend. We had Archbishop Nzimbi in Kenya, along with the Ugandan, Nigerian, and Australian archbishops. When I found GAFCON, I felt at home. It was almost like the East African Revival. Brethren who could condemn sin. When they visited my diocese, they did not introduce themselves as partners. For me, GAFCON is the place for anyone who wants to remain faithful to Scripture and remain Anglican. GAFCON is growing. The liberals are shrinking. Here I can grow the church, here I can stand genuinely. My spirit is at peace. This is the faith I can die for. Your soul and pastoral work will be safe in GAFCON not Canterbury. Think of the missionaries who came to die for the gospel here, and Jesus who died on the cross and was resurrected.

Bishop 9. Why do churches disagree? That should be the first question. They disagree because there are issues entering the Church that are not scriptural. When this happens, disagreements are inevitable. We should go back to the Scriptures. Let us go back to the basics. Why are we disagreeing when we are baptized and confirmed? It is because of unhappy developments worming their way into the Communion.

ANALYSIS: PROSPECTS AND PROBLEMS

Influential as religious leaders may be, individuals do not necessarily reflect the attitudes of the larger groups to which they belong. The interviews illustrate a range of discussion among bishops in Kenya. It is not possible to generalize from these remarks to all Kenyan Anglicans. However, the interviews suggest some aspects of the debate that have been suppressed amid posturing between different parties. Specifically, while a significant number of bishops in Africa and Kenya are fed up with the challenges facing the Communion, this is not universally true. In our interviews, the same person, in some cases, would move back and forth between confrontation and conciliation. As ever, religious and social factors are deeply intertwined, and contexts rapidly evolve.

First and foremost, bishops inclined toward conciliation focused on bridge building, and tended to invoke tolerance, listening, fellowship, dialogue, networking, sharing, diversity, forgiveness, and reconciliation. Such language points to a great desire for continued life together in communion, even when it involves challenges. The

Anglican family should leverage these bishops for the purpose of repairing and strengthening our broken relationships. While considerable attention has been given to attempting to listen to voices that seek to disengage from the Anglican family, not much structured attention has been given to other voices, both in order to gain insight into the complexities around the sexuality debate and to pursue possible paths of reconciliation.

Second, some of the bishops interviewed expressed concerns with what they perceived as lack of magnanimity toward differences in the Communion. This concern was framed as a need to extend pastoral care to those who may be different from "us." Such pastoral care is not seen necessarily as expressive of agreement with certain positions but rather as a gospel invitation to forgiveness and reconciliation. Related here was a commitment to preserving and building our unity as a Communion through linkages and networks.

Third, the interviews illustrated a growing fatigue with the sexuality debate and a desire for the Communion to focus on the gospel in its fullness. Within the Kenyan context, more pressing issues are numerous, including an urgent need to address the political and governmental sphere, climate change, poverty, and human trafficking, as well as to tend properly to theological education, catechesis, and evangelism. On all counts, the call is to pay attention to the whole world, not least in its suffering, and to embrace a communion of common action. If there is an ecclesiological kernel here, it is to invest in the Anglican Communion, such that we may find it capable of managing conflicts that may threaten to break us apart. Our common witness does not require uniformity but a kind of Pentecostal diversity.

Fourth and finally, some bishops adopted a confrontational

stance over against what they call a liberal accommodation of sin, and concomitant persecution of the orthodox in service of a homosexual agenda. During our conversations in the House of Bishops, some suggested that we do not need communion with Canterbury in order to be Anglicans. Such voices, which I take to be extreme, show that leaders can easily slip into a sectarian mode of engagement, according to which polemical engagement of the other predominates. Here, the other is the mainstream Anglican Communion itself, and its historical structures.

HOPE FOR THE FUTURE

Even in this last case, however, and certainly in the first three, we can and should find openings for intercultural conversation amid difference and disagreement. This is a theological hope, based on the conviction that when the Church faces new challenges, God ensures that the gospel will shed new light upon our pressing questions, precisely in and through engagement of one another. The unity to which Christ calls us passes through our differences on the way to their resolution and reconciliation. *In communion*, we learn both to transcend and transform disagreement. Embracing and celebrating our differences of culture and worldview, we seek to make a fresh approach to Christian truth and, by God's grace, agree.

The challenges the Anglican Communion is facing present an opportunity to look afresh at foundational traditions, and what holds them together. While Anglicanism is not defined by fixed doctrinal formulae in all situations, we should commit to a process and a means by which we can navigate tensions in varied circumstances. An important reason why the problems about sexuality have escalated is that it appears to the Kenyan bishops that there has been no serious attempt to offer an explanation to, or consult meaningfully with, the Communion as a whole about the theological reasons that could justify recent moves by some dioceses and provinces.

Here, indeed, we need a structure or model to mediate resolution. In African contexts, we speak of *family ties* to refer to close associations by virtue of common ancestry. Extended families embrace a number of generations and are united by strong and enduring bonds. These close ties nurture family members through trials and difficulties and are a source of inspiration and love. Even when two brothers are engaged in a physical fight, our culture provides avenues for restoring the family relationship.

By analogy, the family of the Church cannot—should not—be broken easily by circumstances. The family of God comprises those suffering trials, temptations, and times of crisis, all of which we hope and expect to engage with goodness and kindness, justice and truth. Anglicans, as one family of Christians, should expect to find grace-filled renewal as we share more fully the delights and sufferings of all in the family. In this, as in all things, we will find our common future in the singular security of God's promise to his people (Gen. 12.1-2; Matt. 16:18). Striving together in the Spirit, let us lay claim to that future by responding in new ways to the call of the gospel, even amid disagreement and failure. The way of resolution will be marked by faith, hope, and love.

SEVEN

Charles Henry Brent's Way of Unity

Faith and Order Origins

R. William Franklin

The topic of disagreement in the Church naturally compels us to consider figures who have navigated the frothy waters of discord in their own time and context and managed neatly, if no doubt narrowly, to avoid the shoals of division. In this essay, I focus on Bishop Charles Henry Brent (1862-1929), Bishop of Western New York and a pioneering ecumenist, among much else. Brent's experiences on the front lines of disagreement inspired him to form the Faith and Order Movement, which became a global instrument of organized theological dialogue as a path to unity. Brent's personal and vocational journey are ripe with wisdom and guidance for all Anglicans who seek today what Brent sought a century ago: the preservation and/or recovery of unity amid disagreement.

We tend to separate the concepts that have come to fuel the Ecumenical Movement from the personal stories, internal psychology, and struggles that have formed its leaders. In the case of Brent (as no doubt for many others), to excise the personal is to miss much of what motivated his vision and enabled his success. Out of turmoil and confusion Brent was endowed with wisdom, patience, and a reconciling temper. In episodes of stress, conflict, and challenge, he perceived that disagreement was the primary factor in opposition to God's will of *unity* for the Church. As we shall see, Brent forged his personal experiences of confrontation, abuse of power, and disappointment into instruments of conciliation, grace, and purpose to achieve his constant goal of unity. Out of struggle emerged the three defining characteristics of Brent's personality that ultimately shaped a world-wide movement: his commitment to surrender to God's will, which gave him independence of thought and action; his desire to be equally at home with the rich and the poor; and his courage to face opposition from those in power and to challenge those he thought wrong.

There are extensive Brent archives in the Diocese of Western New York and the Library of Union Theological Seminary in New York City, in addition to the 13,450 Brent papers in the Library of Congress. Yet we have only one, abbreviated biography of Brent by a former dean of Virginia Theological Seminary, Alexander Zabriskie. There is much, therefore, to explore of Bishop Brent's legacy. In this essay, I will provide a short account of his vocational journey and achievements; identify the key episodes of disagreement with which Brent contended that shaped his person and psychology; and finally consider how those experiences culminated in the formation and stewardship of the Faith and Order Movement.

ARC OF A LIFE

When I arrived in Buffalo as a latter-day Bishop of New York, I found that Bishop Brent's work was largely forgotten. This surprised me, given his prolific involvement in the Episcopal Church. He was eclipsed in collective memory, perhaps, by the showier, genteel Lauristan I. Scaife, Seventh Bishop to the Diocese and wealthy scion of the politically conservative Pittsburgh Scaife/Mellon family. Unlike Bishop Scaife, who was chauffeured everywhere, Brent made use of the driving lessons he received from General Pershing around the battlefields of France and drove himself to parish visitations. He maintained an ambitious schedule, which often saw him racing from one engagement to another. Among his numerous episcopal achievements, he also holds the dubious record of collecting more traffic tickets than any other elected official in New York State in the 1920's. In 1925 he made the papers when, on a return trip from Niagara Falls, he T-boned a streetcar and was subsequently arrested and incarcerated. He was able to make the bail of ten dollars and carry on—clad the while in vestments that he had not removed for fear of being late to his meeting.

Brent was an immigrant, born to an Anglican parish priest and a homemaker in the village of Newcastle in Canada on the shores of Lake Ontario. From these humble beginnings, Brent first made his way to Buffalo as a curate in 1887. Brent's daily life and ascent in the Episcopal Church were conducted at an electric pace. Prior to his tenure in Buffalo, he was elected first Missionary Bishop to the Philippine Islands in 1901. In 1909 he was named president of the first International Opium Commission in Shanghai and served in the same role of the Second International Opium Commission in the Hague in 1911. He was Chief of Chaplains of the American Expeditionary Forces in France from 1917-1919.

Brent accepted election as diocesan in Western New York in 1917, when Buffalo was the eighth largest city in the United States, with a booming industrial economy. In addition, he was twice elected Bishop of Washington, D.C., once elected Bishop of New Jersey, and he came in second on the 14th and last ballot of the first election of a Presiding Bishop of the Episcopal Church (John Gardner Murray of Maryland was elected) in 1925. He refused election in Washington and New Jersey because he felt his ministry in the Philippines was not finished, and he was defeated as Presiding Bishop because he advocated Episcopal Church membership in the new Federal Council of Churches, which was a largely Protestant affair.

He functioned as Bishop-in-Charge of the American Episcopal Churches in Europe in 1926-1928. He contributed two collects to the 1928 Book of Common Prayer (which carried over to the 1979 book), one on welcome and the other on unity. He published 20 books, and picked up honorary doctorates from Harvard, Yale, Columbia, Glasgow, Toronto, and other institutions. His picture appeared on the cover of *Time* in August 1927 at the conclusion of the World Conference on Faith and Order. And he managed throughout his life to excel in physically demanding sports like cricket, polo, hockey, and tennis.

As an Episcopal bishop he refused to be pigeonholed. He was an Anglo-Catholic who introduced the Anglican Missal to the parishes of the Philippines, yet he opposed Anglo-Catholic disdain of mainstream ecumenism. He encouraged the invocation of the saints and the reservation of the Blessed Sacrament for ministration to the sick, and yet he did not believe liturgy in the Episcopal Church should be restricted to the Book of Common Prayer.

Amid numerous roles, responsibilities, and appointments, Brent founded the Faith and Order Movement in 1910. He served as its first president and was the chief inspiration for its mission until his death in 1929. The Faith and Order Movement, we may recall, "serves the Churches by leading them into theological dialogue as a means to overcome obstacles to, and opening up ways towards, the manifestation of their unity given in Jesus Christ."[1] From its nascency, Brent "exercised a profound influence" and remained a loyal servant to the cause, serving as president of the first World Conference on Faith and Order in Lausanne, Switzerland, in 1927.[2] 400 participants, representing officially 127 Anglican, Orthodox, and Protestant Churches met under the leadership of Brent with the objective, officially, "to register the apparent level of fundamental agreements within the Conference and the grave points of disagreement remaining."[3]

---

1   *Dictionary of the Ecumenical Movement*, ed. Nicholas Lossky et al. (Geneva: WCC Publications, 1991), 411. I wish to thank the following colleagues for their generous contributions to this chapter: Judy Stark, Susan Witt, Pierre Whalon, Tom Ely, Stephen Holton, Massimo De Giocchino, and the staff of the Burke Library of Union Theological Seminary in New York City.

2   *Ibid.*

3   *Ibid.*, 412.

FORMATIVE EPISODES

Brent's vision for moving to fundamental agreements from grave points of disagreement was forged from his experiences of dealing with distinctive crises throughout his life. These crises illustrate how Brent's vision and approach to disagreement helped to shape the Faith and Order Movement.

1. Response to a Bishop's Ultimatum

By the time Brent graduated from Trinity College at the University of Toronto in 1884, the seed of Anglo-Catholicism had been planted in him. After three more years spent in his native Canada without receiving a call to parish ministry, he moved across Lake Ontario to Buffalo and was appointed curate-in-charge of St. Andrew's Mission. That same summer he also attended a retreat for clergy conducted by the Rev. A.C.A. Hall, the Superior of the American Province of the Cowley Fathers, a modern Anglican monastic order that had emerged from the Oxford Movement. Hall, an English immigrant, became a close friend and the chief spiritual influence on Brent, encouraging him toward an advanced ritualism that brought a sacramental dimension to social justice. Brent immediately placed candles on the altar of St. Andrew's to bring a greater sense of warmth and the beauty of holiness of those gathered for worship.

The second bishop of Western New York, Arthur Cleveland Coxe, a moderate high churchman, forbade candles on the altar as too "Popish." Likewise, he was fearful of the large number of Roman Catholic immigrants pouring into Buffalo whom he defined as "vast and mongrel."[4] Was it not also their Southern and Eastern European origins that was a source of dismay—Italians, Poles, and Czechs? Coxe determined that in these "uncertain times," no altar candles would be allowed and that Brent would be fired if they were not removed. Brent promptly resigned, showing the vein of non-conformity that, perhaps ironically, would serve to make him an effective ecumenical mediator. Brent's biographer writes, "It is possible that some of his patience with impetuous or difficult clergymen was due to the lifelong impression made upon him by his break with Bishop Coxe."[5] As an ecumenist, Brent rejected ultimatums issued by denominations.

2. Response to a Monastic Superior's Ultimatum

Brent left Buffalo and moved to Boston in 1888, drawn by an opportunity to serve under his new friend Hall at the Church of St. John the Baptist, a mission of the Cowley Fathers. Hall's theology was a liberal Anglo-Catholicism merged with commitment to the Social Gospel, and he drew into his circle a cadre of young intellectuals, including Ralph Adams Cram, the greatest Episcopal architect of the twentieth century. Hall baptized Cram. Brent stood as godfather.

This circle was also drawn into friendship with Phillips Brooks, the rector of Trinity Church, Copley Square, and the greatest

---

4   Elizabeth A. Clark, *Founding the Fathers: Early Church History and Protestant Professors in Nineteenth-Century America* (Philadelphia: University of Pennsylvania Press, 2011), 86.

5   Alexander C. Zabriskie, *Bishop Brent: A Crusader for Christian Unity* (Philadelphia: Westminster Press, 1948), 25.

Episcopal preacher of the nineteenth century. Also formed by the Social Gospel, Brooks undoubtedly served as the spiritual leader of Boston in the waning days of its WASP ascendancy. For these reasons, Brooks was elected Bishop of Massachusetts in 1891. Conservative Anglo-Catholics sought to block the confirmation of his election, on grounds of Brooks's theological liberalism. As a member of the Standing Committee of the Diocese of Massachusetts, Hall endorsed Brooks's election, and vigorously and publicly supported his consecration. For this, Hall was recalled to Oxford and fired as the American Superior of the Cowley Fathers. Brent traveled to England with Hall, stood with him through his ordeal, and, on reflection, shook the dust of monasticism from his feet forever.

This second experience of ecclesiastical tyranny thrust Brent into a depression bordering on despair. Hall, now returned to America, was elected as Bishop of Vermont in 1894 and continued as the chief influence on Brent for the rest of Brent's life. Hall's rise from the shame of defeat taught Brent self-mastery and a conquest over his own volatile personality and turbulent inner life: a hard victory strongly influenced by Hall's "Gospel of Friendship," with its invitation to the construction of a beloved sacramental community.[6]

6 For a detailed description of Hall's "Gospel of Friendship" and his circle, see Douglas Shand-Tucci, *Boston Bohemia, 1881-1900, Volume One of Ralph Adams Cram: Life and Architecture* (Amherst: University of Massachusetts Press, 1995), 192-193. For a standard biography of Hall, see George Lynde Richardson, *Arthur C.A. Hall, Third Bishop of Vermont* (Boston: Houghton Mifflin Company, 1932).

3. Response to a Bishop's Assignment to a Slum Parish

In 1891 Bishop Brooks placed Brent and another former Cowley priest, the Rev. Henry Torbert, in charge as co-rectors of what became one such sacramental community, an abandoned church in the slums of South East Boston. Brent was now 29 and finally able to keep a steady job for the next decade.

His struggling parish was St. Stephen's, in a neighborhood crowded with marginalized people. Though the Roman Catholic Irish were now ascendant and in charge of the city, including South Boston, some Episcopalians found energy for social engagement. Amid hardship Brent was able to create a diverse and vibrant gathering place for people on the precipice of poverty. He provided schools, wages, shelter, and social clubs, and became much loved by many, not least the Harvard undergraduates who helped with Brent's boys' clubs, athletic teams, and job fairs. From this socially-minded ferment sprang settlement house workers like Vida Scudder, who during Brent's tenure founded, from St. Stephen's, the Episcopal Church Socialist League.

How did Brent, who had been marked in some ways by Anglo-Catholic party fervor, attract these radical reformers? By bringing together people of varying perspectives in whom he did not perceive irreconcilable disagreement. In this way, he blended Tractarian and Puseyite theologies of the cross and Eucharist with the Social Gospel. His mission was to revitalize all South Boston by immersing it in the sacramental, liturgical, and devotional life. At St. Stephen's, Torbert and Brent used ritualistic services of color, light, and pageantry to inspire such a societal renewal.[7]

Historian Robert Prichard suggests that this achievement in the slums of Boston, cross-pollinating Episcopal parties, helped inspire Brent's call as a bishop. In his book *With God in the World* (1899), Brent called for an amalgamation of home missions, which had been the work of the Anglo-Catholic party, with foreign missions, which had been the work of the Evangelical party. Together they would form a united missionary enterprise, an idea that attracted the attention of the House of Bishops and led to his election as missionary bishop to the Philippine Islands in 1901.

4. Response to a Dehumanizing Imperialism

1901 was a landmark year for the establishment of new missionary districts, and the reach of the Episcopal Church was formally extended to Puerto Rico, the Philippines, and Honolulu, Hawaii. For the Episcopal Church, it was a time of opportunity. For the Philippine Islands, it was a period of recovery after a bloody four-year war and transition to becoming the first United States colony.

On the one hand, Brent had a positive attitude toward American imperialism. He trusted that the United States could bring the best of a democratic civilization to an "unenlightened" nation.[8] On the other

---

7 For an excellent study of Brent's theology of cross, sacrament, and social justice, see Arun W. Jones, *Christian Missions in the American Empire* (Frankfurt am Main: Peter Lang, 2003).

8 Ian T. Douglas, *Fling Out the Banner: The National Church Ideal and the Foreign Mission of the Episcopal Church* (New York: The Church Hymnal Corporation, 1996), 74. For recent studies that discuss Brent and

hand, he feared an American expansionism that would import into an Asian land the worst aspects of capitalism, evangelical Protestantism, and white supremacy in imperialistic guise.

This caution did not prevent him from serving as pastor to government officials. He installed in his Manila cathedral a pew of sufficient size and strength to support the 450-pound heft of the governor, William Howard Taft, who quickly became an active Episcopalian and would go on to serve as the 27th president of the United States. In 1910, Brent confirmed the commander of U.S. forces, John J. Pershing, and he led hundreds of other U.S. officials into the Episcopal Church. In 1917 Pershing would appoint Brent as chief U.S. Chaplain to American forces in Europe. At the same time, Brent observed that sharp disagreement among the various denominations weakened the Christian witness in Asia. The desperately needed antidote was a united Christendom in the mission field. Brent applied the policy of cooperation, not conversion, that he had adopted in Boston, encouraging other Christians to become better members of their own communions.

The Philippines had been a Roman Catholic, Spanish colony for four hundred years, served primarily by a powerful Franciscan order. In 1903 the Catholic Church followed Episcopal playbook and appointed an American, Dennis Dougherty, to be the Bishop of Nueva Segovia in the Philippines. Dougherty had studied at the

---

imperialism, see Andrew Preston, *Sword of the Spirit, Shield of the Faith* (New York and Toronto: Alfred A. Knopf, 2012), Rebecca Tinio McKenna, *American Imperial Pastoral* (Chicago: University of Chicago Press, 2017), and Susan K. Harris, *God's Arbiters* (Oxford: Oxford University Press, 2017).

North American College in Rome, and was among the new breed of "Romanizing" American bishops. Brent maintained cordial relations with Dougherty and opposed the Evangelical Protestant strategy of aggressively seeking Roman Catholic conversions. Brent still worried about the Philippine Franciscans, however. As Zabriskie writes, Brent "became convinced that the Roman priesthood was deeply infected by dishonesty and immorality—much more than the clergy of any other church—and therefore but little likely to lead people to lives of integrity and purity."[9] Even so, Brent accepted that "Rome was part of the Church of Christ, and he would not be a partner to any activity directed against it."[10] At this time, he initiated a lifelong practice of working as closely as possible with the Catholic Church, though he believed that the unreformed Rome (decades prior to Vatican II) "had absolutely no intention of doing anything constructive toward unity."[11]

Brent also declined to pursue anything resembling coercive conversion of the indigenous people of the Philippines. Working among the hill people far from Manila, especially the Moros and the Igorots, Brent developed an indigenous ecclesiology that transformed his attitude toward mission. As he later reflected, "it was among the pagan peoples that I learned the equality before God of all men, which I count to be the chief treasure I have honestly made my own in my lifetime."[12]

---

9   Zabriskie, *Brent,* 143.

10   *Ibid.,* 144.

11   *Ibid.,* 146.

12   F. W. Kater, *Things That Matter: The Best of the Writings of Bishop Brent* (New York: Harper and Brothers, 1949), 6.

5. Response to the Dehumanization of War

On his election in Western New York, Brent did not take residence for nearly two years in order to serve as chaplain of the American Expeditionary Force in World War I. He supervised, organized, and pastored the 1,300 U.S. chaplains of all faiths on the front lines, and learned to drive ambulances under the tutelage of General Pershing.

He was once again transformed, this time by the brutality of a war that bore witness to the utter inability of the churches to intervene and prevent the loss of fifteen million lives. At the same time, the witness of thousands of chaplains working together in common cause became a "living fact and a great symbol." As he wrote at the time, "the sole hope for peace" is the fact that "the horrors of war and its savagery increase... unity of heart and hands among the churches."[13] Arriving to his new home, Brent brought fragmentary pieces of the cathedrals of France shattered by German cannon fire and placed them on the interior walls of St. Paul's Cathedral in Buffalo to remind worshippers of the price of disagreement, and of the call of the Eucharist to visible communion in Christ.

6. Response to an Ecumenical Ultimatum

The end of World War I brought appeals for unity by several churches, including Lambeth Conference 1920's "Appeal to All Christian People." Brent was part of a small working group of four bishops

---

13 Zabriskie, *Brent*, 152. Cf. Archives of the Episcopal Diocese of Western New York (Tonawanda, NY), Brent Folders, MS F.W. Kates, Bishop Brent: Adventurer on Uncharted Seas, 3-4.

who drafted the appeal in one afternoon gathered in the garden of Lambeth Palace. Based on the four points of the Chicago-Lambeth Quadrilateral of 1888, the appeal proved influential in its passionate call for the visible unity of all Christians, and its imaginative re-presentation of a historic episcopate locally adapted that all churches may be able to embrace. Many early ecumenical conversations drew inspiration from the appeal, and its main lines of argument also set the terms of Anglican ecclesiology for the next century. And yet, early hopes for a broad ecumenical reception of the historic episcopate—even in the broadened terms of *episcopé*, as proposed in *Baptism, Eucharist and Ministry* (1982), in the train of the 1920 Lambeth appeal—were likely too optimistic. Brent himself, on reflection, wondered about the proffered methodology, weaknesses of which were raised by representatives of the English so-called non-conformist churches from in the 1920s. These discussions "reaching a significant level of agreement but founder[ed] on the Anglican requirement of episcopal ordination in a United Church."[14] The appeal's disapproval of inter-communion and the exchange of pulpits also struck a painful note, as did the ever-present specter of "validity" of orders, a category that has bedeviled inter-church encounter since the dawn of the ecumenical movement.[15]

---

14 Charlotte Methuen, "The Making of 'An Appeal to All Christian People' at the 1920 Lambeth Conference," in *The Lambeth Conference: Theology, History, Polity, and Purpose*, ed. Paul Avis and Benjamin Guyer (London: Bloomsbury, 2017), 130.

15 See Henry Chadwick, "The Quadrilateral in England," in *Quadrilateral at One Hundred*, ed. J. Robert Wright (London: Mowbrays, 1988), 149.

ORIGINS OF THE FAITH
AND ORDER MOVEMENT

Bishop Brent looked to the Faith and Order Movement to advance the ecumenical cause. The term *Faith and Order* first appears in the Chicago Quadrilateral passed by the House of Bishops at the 1886 General Convention. As the text affirms, the Episcopal Church does not seek to "absorb other Communions, but rather, co-operating with them on the basis of a common Faith and Order, to discountenance schism, to heal the wounds of the Body of Christ, and to promote the charity which is the chief of Christian graces and the visible manifestation of Christ to the world." Moreover, the bishops continued, "we do hereby affirm that Christian unity can be restored only by the return of all Christian Communions to the principles of unity exemplified by the undivided Catholic Church during the first ages of its existence; which principles we believe to be the substantial deposit of Christian Faith and Order committed by Christ and his Apostles to the Church."[16]

Brent's first use of *Faith and Order* came at the World Missionary Conference of 1910 in Edinburgh. This meeting, given to the articulation of strategy by missionary executives from multiple denominations, issued organically in the hope for a unified, pan-Protestant evangelization of the world. Archbishop William Temple, for his part, would later criticize the conference for deliberately excluding "points of difference" from the discussions in order to achieve the

---

16   The Book of Common Prayer (1979), 877.

goal of unity.[17] There was truth in this. Brent believed, however, that "the sense of God's presence at that conference, and the wonderful and immediate results, ... led some of us to believe that a similar conference on matters of faith and order might be productive of good.... At the morning Eucharist there came vividly before me the possibility of a world Conference on Faith and Order."[18] Thus was born in the sacrament, and continued in prayer, as Brent would later say, his vision for the world conference would in fact start from points of differences, the address of which would promote progress in unity.[19] And he believed *all* of Christendom, including the Roman Catholic and Orthodox churches, should be present.

Monumentally, at the 1910 General Convention of the Episcopal Church meeting in Cincinnati, Brent persuaded the convention to establish a Joint Commission to Promote a World Conference on Faith and Order. Its "definite purpose" would be to consider "those things in which we differ, in the hope that a better understanding of divergent views of Faith and Order will result in a deepened desire for reunion and an official action on the part of the separate Communions

---

17 Archives of the Burke Library at Union Theological Seminary (New York, NY), William Brown Adams Papers, Folder 1, MS William Temple, The Faith and Order Meeting, 1935.

18 Archives of Western New York, Brent Folders, MS Charles Brent, A Pilgrimage Toward Unity: Report of Plan on World Conference, 1920, 14; MS F. W. Kates, Bishop Brent, 4.

19 See Burke Library Archives, MS William Temple, The Faith and Order Meeting, 20.

themselves."[20] Of course, the movement would need to extend beyond the Protestant world. Thus Brent also urged the convention to suggest that leaders of all churches, responsibly appointed, meet for patient discussion of those matters of faith (doctrine and beliefs) and order (polity and governance). Brent was appointed as chair of General Convention's first Joint Commission on Approaches to Unity.

FROM IDEAS TO ACTION

In 1911, the Joint Commission established a permanent office in Boston directed by a secretary, Robert H. Gardiner, an Episcopal layman, whose keen, legally-trained mind was eager to turn ideas into a plan. Brent toured the world to recruit supporters—above all his friend the Archbishop of Canterbury, Randall Davidson, and his financial backer for the project, J.P. Morgan. Traveling through mountains and crossing oceans, Brent scribbled his thoughts in notebooks and Gardiner turned them into pamphlets. It was said that Faith and Order was the work of a lawyer, a banker, and a prophet. They reached out to "all Christian Communions throughout the World which confess Jesus Christ as Lord and Saviour."[21] By 1920, Faith and Order Commissions had been appointed by 69 participating churches.

A preliminary conference on Faith and Order, attended by 70 official representatives from 49 nations, met in Geneva in 1920 in

---

20   John E. Skoglund and J. Robert Nelson, *Fifty Years of Faith and Order* (New York: Committee for the InterSeminary Movement, 1963), 15.

21   Skoglund and Nelson, *Fifty Years*, 16.

the wake of World War I and the Lambeth Conference's appeal. Brent called the conference to order, was elected its president, and gave the opening address, but the conference as a whole took the responsibility for organizing a next meeting, governed now by continuation and business committees. Other leaders also emerged, notably John R. Mott, the Methodist sparkplug for the World's Student Christian Federation; Peter Ainslee, the influential Disciples of Christ spokesman; William Adams Brown, a Presbyterian from Union Theological Seminary; and a new financial backer, Baptist layman John D. Rockefeller.

The First World Conference on Faith and Order met in Lausanne, Switzerland, August 3-21, 1927, and was attended by 400 official delegates from 40 nations representing 127 autonomous churches, both Protestant and Eastern Orthodox , including Russians. The Southern Baptists and Missouri Synod Lutherans stayed away; Roman Catholics participated as unofficial observers. Brent presided, assisted the while by a vice-president, Alfred Garvie, the Congregationalist professor beloved for his marked Scottish accent and sense of humor. Brent preached on the call to unity at the opening service in Lausanne Cathedral. Sessions were held in the Great Hall of the University of Lausanne. Every day a team of translators and stenographers had the minutes of the morning sessions available in mimeographed form in three languages by the time the afternoon sessions began.[22]

---

22 A complete original set of these mimeographed minutes may be found in the Burke Library Archives at Union.

ALMOST DERAILED

The greatest disagreement at Lausanne arose with respect to a proposed final Section VII of the draft report, entitled "The Unity of Christendom and the Relation Thereto to Existing Churches." It was meant to set forth what could be said about the characteristics of a united Church and what action could be taken for unity following the conference. Largely the work of Archbishop Nathan Soderblom of Stockholm, the section controversially urged that rapid steps be taken toward inter-communion, among other things. Catholic-minded delegates to the conference worried that Section VII embraced a vision of an overly broad Church, compromised regarding both episcopal office and affirmation of the Nicene creed. Bishop Charles Gore of Oxford, an influential theologian and founder of a monastic order, made clear that the report as written would make his future participation in Faith and Order impossible, because it lacked fundamental elements of the catholic faith. Bishop William Manning of New York, an original proposer of Faith and Order to the Episcopal Church, likewise found the report unacceptably slanted toward a Protestant, Life and Work perspective (the latter having emerged two years prior at a meeting in Stockholm). Redoubtable Episcopal ecumenist, editor of *The Living Church*, and principal drafter of section VI of the report, Dr. F.C. Morehouse, rose amid the final session to make the awkward motion that the draft section VII be referred back to the Continuation Committee that would now oversee Faith and Order. Morehouse's speech was "received with consternation."[23]

---

23 Zabriskie, *Bishop Brent*, 171.

Widespread confusion broke out. Several other representatives of churches now rose to press particular shades of belief that differentiated them from the report, and to state that because of these they could not sign. A second draft changed no minds. Bishop Brent, however, "in the most gracious way, suggested from the platform that, under the circumstances, Mr. Morehouse's resolution undoubtedly presented the best way out of the difficulty."[24] Dr. Garvie concurred, as did Bishop Gore, the Archbishop of Armagh, and others. At the critical moment, Brent remained composed and serene, never hurried, providing needed assurances that no one's convictions would be overridden. Section VII thus disappeared into the mists of Church history, leaving section one to six—on the call to unity, the Church's message to the world, the nature of the Church, the Church's common confession of faith, the ministry, and the sacraments to be voted on and received unanimously.

Brent's decisive and gracious presidency over the conference explains his appearance on the cover of *Time* magazine eight days later. It was Brent's greatest and last moment of Faith and Order leadership. The seemingly unstoppable man, worn out, died 18 months later. Hard-won and costly, Brent's achievement at Lausanne epitomized his approach to managing disagreement on the way to unity, which was a lifetime in the making.

---

24 W. Bertrand Stevens, *Editor's Quest: A Memoir of Frederic Cook Morehouse* (New York: Morehouse-Gorham, 1940), 219.

MODEL FOR THE CHURCH

What is Brent's legacy for us? Ultimately, Brent developed a comparative ecclesiology on an ecumenical foundation, properly flexible and comprehending four types or forms of worship: (1) a strictly controlled, historically rich liturgy; (2) silent meditation, interspersed with brief teaching; (3) non-liturgical worship, constructed from contemporary materials; and (4) revivalism. Brent held these together within a broad doctrinal latitude. Structurally, Brent preferred personal ties to organic or legislative ones. In a future united Church, Christ the King would serve as head of a single structure, within which distinct denominations might find a home.

If the end is full visible unity, the means can only be a patient process of reconciliation, which Brent believed would be achieved by "conference." Conference would, in the first place, identify points of fundamental faith upon which sufficient agreement has been reached such that they no longer divide. Second, conference would, in the very process of consultation and conversation, provide a means by which to distinguish essentials from preferences, prejudices, and organizational conveniences. On both counts, the *way* of conference interested Brent enormously, that is, the synodical style of meetings between leaders. In *Pilgrimage Toward Unity,* published in advance of the preliminary meeting on Faith and Order, Brent describes the process as "sympathetic interchange of thought," personal, and respectful, as distinct from controversialist attacks, which tend toward self-orientation. In this way, conference might prepare the way for a genuine "Council" of several communions of churches, none of which would be supreme. "Christian Communions now separated from one another will retain in a United Church much of their distinctive character," wrote Brent. "It is in inclusion and disciplined diversity that the unity of the whole fellowship will be fulfilled."[25]

The 1927 Conference in Lausanne presented the first real test of this model. A few months before, Brent wrote to the American Committee on Faith and Order of his hopes for the work, which should employ, he said, a comparative methodology. Theologians would humbly sit at a "common table" with others and "try to discover the flaws in his own ideas and the virtues in those of his fellows." Employing a "language of friendship," leaders would strive "to see sympathetically what is in the mind of another that you may give him all the credit that is due to the truth of his position." A certain *love* enters in here, said Brent, through which we may hope to reach "common understanding on great truths."[26]

Looking ahead, it is hard to overemphasize the extent to which we still need to learn these lessons and pursue a consultative, consensus-oriented synodality of common life in the Church. If the heyday of ecumenism has anything to teach us, it is that we are never through with the holy work of overcoming our isolation and egocentrism as distinct churches, all too happy to walk apart from the one visible Body. To discover that the gospel is greater and more complex than hitherto believed is humbling but necessary. "We are here at the urgent behest

25 All from Charles H. Brent, *A Pilgrimage Toward Unity* (Geneva: Faith and Order, 1920), 19-20.

26 Archives of Western New York, Brent Folders, MS Charles Henry Brent, Address to the American Committee on the World Conference on Faith and Order, November 29, 1926, 3 and 5.

of Jesus Christ," declared Brent in the opening address at Lausanne. To answer the Lord's summons was, and remains, a holy work, the doing of which enlivens the People of God and enacts the good news of reconciliation for all nations, tongues, tribes, and peoples.[27]

27 I here follow W.A. Visser 't Hooft's inspiring reflection, "The 1927 Lausanne Conference in Retrospect," in *Lausanne 77: Fifty Years of Faith and Order*, ed. Lukas Vischer (Geneva: World Council of Churches, 1977), 19-20.

EIGHT

Architecture
of Authority

John Bauerschmidt

INTRODUCTION

Is it possible for churches to disagree on important points of teaching and, at the same time, to sustain some degree of communion with each other? The question touches, in significant part, on authority, as a necessary means of adjudicating disputed issues. And it concerns the nature of *communion* itself, as that which the churches share, notwithstanding the dispute. On both counts, determinations must be made, an authoritative word spoken.

Anglicans have considered questions about authority from the very beginning of the independent course set for the English Church in the 16th century, before there even was an "Anglicanism." These questions were explicit in the various acts of Parliament that limited appeals to the pope and established the authority of King Henry VIII as supreme head on earth of the Church of England. Our own approach to authority can hardly be settled, however, by Henry VIII. The growth of the Church of England, through British colonial expansion and mission work in other parts of the globe (including in the post-colonial Protestant Episcopal Church in the newly constituted United States) has created a new context.

The new churches organized in the wake of this expansion have, by their very existence, raised new issues of authority. How do the several churches with a common English lineage relate to each other? What are the lines of authority? These questions were implicit in the organization of the Episcopal Church, with implications that became clearer over time.

In the 19th century, a new context emerged again, as new Anglican churches round the world sought to preserve and strengthen their relationships with the Church of England and with each other, and to seek common counsel on shared challenges. The bishops of the churches in communion with the See of Canterbury began to meet together at the invitation of the archbishop at the first Lambeth Conference in 1867. Over the years the agenda has grown to accommodate questions of common mission, common identity, and the wider ecumenical unity of the one Church.

In the second half of the 20th century, the proliferation of autonomous Anglican churches in the newly independent post-colonial Global South massively increased the scope and diversity of the Communion. The churches represented at the Lambeth Conference see themselves as part of a global communion of churches. These churches seek to express a common life and, increasingly, a greater embodiment of unity, catholicity, and apostolicity. New institutions within Anglicanism have arisen to aid in the expression of this common life, chief among them the Anglican Consultative Council and the Primates' Meeting. Along with the Archbishop of Canterbury and the Lambeth Conference, these serve as "instruments of communion," raising again the question of authority. Does the Anglican Consultative Council speak for the Church? Does the Primates' Meeting? Ought these institutions defer to the Lambeth Conference as a prior authority?

This essay considers two key points in history when questions of authority in the Church of England and Anglican Communion were raised and addressed in ways that may prove helpful for our analogous discernments today. First, I will explore how the 16th century Articles of Religion oscillated in their ascription of authority in the church between the Holy Scriptures and the reigning monarch, and deployed *coherence* as a scriptural hermeneutic. Second, I will examine the 1948 Lambeth Conference's Report of the Committee on the Anglican Communion, which significantly and self-consciously defined a "dispersed" authority. Taken together, these two moments in Anglican history helpfully instruct us about the architecture of authority, without which we will have little hope of sustaining sound structures in the Church.

ARTICLES OF RELIGION

The medieval church in England did not possess a centralized authority. Neither the monarch nor the pope held absolute sway, and the bishops did not necessarily see themselves as a collective, acting in lockstep.[1] Rather, a diverse set of overlapping, interlocking authorities—pope and legate, king in parliament, two convocations of Canterbury and York and the metropolitical office of two archbishops, bishops with diocesan jurisdiction, abbots of religious communities, and rectors and vicars of parishes—found themselves arrayed alongside one another. To be sure, final appellate authority in disputed questions was vested in the pope, as was confirmation of episcopal and abbatial elections; the pope's importance was acknowledged in a thousand ways, from mention in the canon of the Mass to regular appeal for dispensations. In practice, however, authority in the medieval church had many centers, not least the monarch.

The English Reformation was an exercise in centralization. The Act of Supremacy of 1534, in Henry's reign, acknowledged the monarch's status as "the only Supreme Head on earth of the Church of England," confirming his possession of "full power and authority... to visit, repress, redress, reform, order, correct, restrain, and amend all such errors, heresies, abuses, offences, contempts, and enormities, whatsoever they may be."[2] Henry appropriated to himself what had

1   G.W. Bernard, *The Late Medieval English Church* (New Haven: Yale University Press, 2012), 47, 65.

2   *Documents of the English Reformation*, ed. Gerald Bray (Minneapolis: Fortress Press, 1995), 114.

been accepted as papal prerogatives (formerly vested in the pope's legate or representative in England, Cardinal Wolsey), uniting this authority with his already extensive power as monarch, to his own end. This legatine power was first vested by the king in the Archbishop of Canterbury, Thomas Cranmer, and then more permanently in the newly created position of vicegerent, held by Thomas Cromwell.[3] A compliant parliament and convocation became the means of enacting the king's will, which was then carried forward for practical implementation by the vicegerent.

Henry VIII's robust articulation of authority over the church in the Tudor period set the stage for continued wrestling with these questions in the Articles of Religion formulated during the reign of his successor, Edward VI. The Articles would be codified in final form during the reign of Elizabeth I, herself the "supreme governor" of the Church of England.

The 39 Articles have endured an uneven reception in Anglicanism. They never defined the Church of England as—what we normally consider—a confessional church, but they were an intrinsic part of the Reformation settlement of religion in England.[4] And though they have occupied less and less prominent a place in subsequent Anglican self-understanding, their clear echo can be heard in Anglican formularies. For instance, recall the statement made by

---

3   Diarmaid MacCulloch, *Thomas Cranmer* (New Haven: Yale University Press, 1996), 125-135.

4   Peter Toon, "The Articles and Homilies" in *The Study of Anglicanism*, rev. edn., ed. Stephen Sykes, John Booty, and Jonathan Knight (Minneapolis: Fortress Press, 1998), 147; Mark Chapman, *Anglican Theology* (London: T&T Clark, 2012), 71.

ordinands in the Episcopal Church, that the Holy Scriptures are "the Word of God" (Article 22 and others) and "contain all things necessary to salvation" (Article 6).[5]

Article 20 says this about the authority of the Church:

> The Church hath power to decree Rites or Ceremonies, and authority in Controversies of Faith: and yet it is not lawful for the Church to ordain any thing that is contrary to God's Word written, neither may it so expound one place of Scripture, that it be repugnant to another. Wherefore, although the Church be a witness and a keeper of Holy Writ, yet, as it ought not to decree any thing against the same, so besides the same ought it not to enforce any thing to be believed for necessity of Salvation.[6]

This article's concern with the relation of the church's authority to the Holy Scriptures is hardly surprising, given that it was forged in the heat of Reformation. It firmly establishes that the church has authority, but it is an authority that may not contradict the Holy Scriptures nor otherwise introduce hermeneutical confusion by pitting one part against another, or adding further precepts regarding salvation where Scripture is silent.

The authority of the church's teaching depends on its coherence with the *whole* of the Holy Scriptures. Article 7, "Of the Old Testament," marks the breadth of the mandate for scriptural coherence in its assertion that "the Old Testament is not contrary to the

---

5   The Book of Common Prayer (1979), 513, 526, 538.

6   *Ibid.*, 871.

New: for both in the Old and New Testament everlasting life is offered to Mankind by Christ, who is the only mediator between God and Man, being both God and Man."[7] The internal coherence of the Holy Scriptures is adumbrated by way of this affirmation of the unity of testaments, a coherence underscored by the longstanding direction at Morning and Evening Prayer to read a chapter or portion of a chapter from both the Old and New Testaments.[8]

Article 34 addresses the church's authority over rites and ceremonies, granting that they need not be the same in every place, and may be changed as needed, as long as nothing is ordained contrary to God's Word (echoing Article 20). Lawfully authorized traditions and ceremonies ought not to be willfully changed by those without authority, but "every particular or national Church hath authority to ordain, change, and abolish, Ceremonies or Rites of the Church ordained only by man's authority, so that all things be done to edifying."[9]

Notably, the Articles lack any specificity as to how authority within the church is to be exercised, and by whom, but Article 37 clearly asserts the princely authority established by Henry VIII: "The King's Majesty hath the chief power in this Realm of England, and other his Dominions, unto whom the chief Government of all Estates of this Realm, whether they be Ecclesiastical or Civil, in all causes doth appertain, and is not, nor ought to be, subject to any foreign Jurisdiction."[10]

---

7   *Ibid.*, 869.

8   BCP 1979, 934; *The Book of Common Prayer: The Texts of 1549, 1559, and 1662*, ed. Brian Cummings (Oxford: Oxford University Press, 2011), 8, 105.

9   BCP 1979, 874.

10   *Ibid.*, 875.

Article 21 adds something more:

General Councils may not be gathered together without the commandment and will of Princes. And when they be gathered together, (forasmuch as they be an assembly of men, whereof all be not governed with the Spirit and Word of God,) they may err, and sometimes have erred, even in things pertaining unto God. Wherefore things ordained by them as necessary to salvation have neither strength nor authority, unless it may be declared that they be taken out of holy Scripture.[11]

The article puts a stake in the ground concerning the power of the monarch in the Church. It stipulates the role of princes in summoning a General Council of the church, namely, that a world-wide gathering of Christians ought not be convened without the call of the reigning monarchs of the Christian world. This may be understood, in part, as a defensive move on the part of the English Church in light of Pope Paul III's convening of the Council of Trent in 1545, which council was still in session when the Articles were first adopted. As Article 37 put it: "The Bishop of Rome hath no jurisdiction in this Realm of England."[12] At the same time, Article 21 may be seen more positively, acknowledging the historic part played by princes in calling the Councils of Constance and Basel in the 15th century, when

11   *Ibid.*, 872.

12   *Ibid.*, 872.

the papacy was contested.[13] In all events, articles 21 and 37 together establish a centralized executive authority in the monarch, subject to "God's Word written" (article 20).

This last is critical: that, while articles 21 and 37 confidently codify monarchical authority, the second part of Article 21 articulates a primacy of Scripture as the most authoritative arbiter. It establishes that a General Council convoked with due princely authority is still bound by the principal of coherence with the Scriptures per Article 20. The point partly recalls the historical claim of article 19, that "as the Church of Jerusalem, Alexandria, and Antioch, have erred, so also the Church of Rome hath erred, not only in their living and manner of Ceremonies, but also in matters of Faith."[14] Councils, in and of themselves, however enabled by princely or papal support, are not guaranteed articulators of truth, except insofar as they cleave to the Holy Scriptures.

We must recall, however, that the Articles of Religion themselves were, at this time, presented as an authoritative text by and within a wider web of established and even competing authorities. The church *in England* has authority; it may speak in a General Council but only one duly called with (English) princely support, under the authority of the Holy Scriptures. The picture is subtle, even reticent, in view of the unfolding English Reformation, in which much is assumed and not articulated. The Articles assume the continued functioning of various kinds of authority in the Church of England. They only

---

13   Francis Oakley, *The Conciliarist Tradition* (Oxford: Oxford University Press, 2003), 38-51.

14   BCP 1979, 871.

refer obliquely to the practical center of power in the Tudor Church, namely, the monarch.

A further complication may be seen in the fact that the unprecedented centralization of the church in the 16th century largely left in place the dispersed administrative authority of the medieval church: dioceses, cathedrals, bishops, convocations, canon law, and ecclesiastical courts. Moreover, Parliament itself would become a less certain tool in the hands of the monarch during the reign of Elizabeth I and her successors, as contestation grew between the monarch and other leaders over the exercise of power and the extent of reform in the church. The concept of the king in parliament as the central executive would, in time, grow to something more resembling modern parliamentary government.

Even so, the English Reformation surely marked a centralization of authority in the church on the part of the Tudor monarchs, in lieu of synodical, representative or consensual government. In principle, ecclesial authority depends on and derives from the Holy Scriptures. Practically, it is administered by the monarch.

LAMBETH CONFERENCE 1948

The 1948 Lambeth Conference, in its report on the Anglican Communion, sets forth an influential articulation of authority in the Communion, in a much different way and under much different circumstances than the Articles of Religion. The 1948 report builds upon the work of the 1930 Lambeth Conference, which was the first to issue a report on the Communion. The 1930 conference adopted resolutions on the Communion, including the definitional Resolution 49:

> The Anglican Communion is a fellowship, within the one Holy Catholic and Apostolic Church, of those duly constituted dioceses, provinces or regional Churches in communion with the See of Canterbury, which have the following characteristics in common: a. they uphold and propagate the Catholic and Apostolic faith and order as they are generally set forth in the Book of Common Prayer as authorised in their several Churches; b. they are particular or national Churches, and, as such, promote within each of their territories a national expression of Christian faith, life and worship; and c. they are bound together not by a central legislative and executive authority, but by mutual loyalty sustained through the common counsel of the bishops in conference.[15]

By this resolution, the 1930 conference laid the groundwork for identifying elements of authority within the Communion, all of which would themselves need defining and elaborating: Catholic and Apostolic faith and order, the Book of Common Prayer, "particular" churches themselves, and common counsel of the bishops in conference. The resolution deprecates "centralized authority," preferring regional autonomy "in communion with the See of Canterbury," another phrase in need of definition.[16]

---

15   *The Lambeth Conference 1930*, Resolution 49 (London: SPCK, 1930), 55; available online.

16   *Ibid.*, 153.

The report of the committee in 1948 continues in the same descriptive mode, but adds an element of prescription as to the relationship of these varied elements. Addressing the question of the Communion's "meaning and unity" at an important juncture in its life, the report emphasizes the Lambeth Conference itself as a means of tending to the relations between Anglican churches, amid a burgeoning ecumenical movement.[17] And the report ventures a brief history of development—from the origin of the Communion in the "national" churches of the British Isles, to its spread overseas, incorporating the rise of missionary societies and founding of first colonial bishoprics. Finally, "under the guidance, and by the power of the Holy Spirit, the Anglican Communion has become today a fellowship of Churches in every part of the world."[18]

Returning to 1930's dismissal of centralization, the 1948 report concurs with previous conferences on decisions not to establish either a formal primacy for Canterbury or an Appellate Tribunal, nor to give the conference legislative powers. Stated positively, "the authority which binds the Anglican Communion together is... moral and spiritual, resting on the truth of the Gospel, and on a charity which is patient and willing to defer to the common mind."[19] Just here, the 1948 report takes the opportunity to venture a more expansive description and defense of an apparently ecumenical vision of authority that the Anglican Communion might seek to enact and share, a non-papal vision rooted in the early Church:

---

17 *The Lambeth Conference 1948* (London: SPCK, 1948), 84.

18 *Ibid.*, 82.

19 *Ibid.*, 84.

Authority, as inherited by the Anglican Communion from the un-divided Church of the early centuries of the Christian era, is single in that it is derived from a single Divine source, and reflects within itself the richness and historicity of the divine Revelation, the authority of the eternal Father, the incarnate Son, and the life-giving Spirit. It is distributed among Scripture, Tradition, Creeds, the Ministry of the Word and Sacraments, the witness of saints, and the *consensus fidelium*, which is the continuing experience of the Holy Spirit through His faithful people in the Church. It is thus a dispersed rather than a centralized authority having many elements which combine, interact with, and check each other; these elements together contributing by a process of mutual support, mutual checking, and redressing of errors or exaggerations to the many-sided fullness of the authority which Christ has committed to His Church. Where this authority of Christ is to be found mediated not in one mode but in several we recognize in this multiplicity God's loving provision against the temptations to tyranny and the dangers of unchecked power.[20]

The report claims that this authority is supple and elastic; that it "releases initiative, trains in fellowship, and evokes a free and willing obedience."[21] It recognizes that such a concept of authority is harder to grasp than that of "a more imperious character," but goes on to claim that it demands a welcome measure of faith.[22] Then it offers a

---

20   *Ibid.,* 85.

21   *Ibid.,* 85.

22   *Ibid.,* 85.

translation, "simple and intelligible," into personal terms:

> God, who is our ultimate personal authority, demands of all His
> creatures entire and unconditional obedience. As in human fam-
> ilies the father is the mediator of this divine authority, so in the
> family of the Church is the bishop, the Father-in-God, wielding
> his authority by virtue of his divine commission and in synodical
> association with his clergy and laity, and exercising it in humble
> submission, as himself under authority.[23]

If, at this point, we start to see the whole picture of authority
as proposed in the report, it becomes necessary to narrate how the
various elements relate to one another. Here, the authors suggest, we
may learn by analogy from the scientific method, which gathers data,
organizes it by formulae, proceeds to publication, and also takes time
to verify by experience. Similarly, "Catholic Christianity presents us
with an organic process of life and thought in which religious experience has been, and is, described, intellectually ordered, mediated, and
verified."[24] More expansively:

> This experience is *described* in Scripture, which is authoritative be-
> cause it is the unique and classical record of the revelation of God
> in His relation to and dealings with man. While Scripture there-
> fore remains the ultimate standard of faith, it should be continually
> interpreted in the context of the Church's life.

23 *Ibid.*, 85.

24 *Ibid.*, 85.

It is *defined* in Creeds and in continuous theological study.

It is *mediated* in the Ministry of the Word and Sacraments, by persons who are called and commissioned by God through the Church to represent both the transcendent and immanent elements in Christ's authority.

It is *verified* in the witness of saints and in the *consensus fidelium*. The Christ-like life carries its own authority, and the authority of doctrinal formulations, by General Councils or otherwise, rests at least in part on their acceptance by the whole body of the faithful, though the weight of this *consensus* does not depend on mere numbers or on the extension of a belief at any one time, but on continuance through the ages, and the extent to which the *consensus* is genuinely free.

This essentially Anglican authority is reflected in our adherence to episcopacy as the source and centre of our order, and the Book of Common Prayer as the standard of our worship. Liturgy, in the sense of the offering and ordering of the public worship of God, is the crucible in which these elements of authority are fused and unified in the fellowship and power of the Holy Spirit. It is the Living and Ascended Christ present in the worshipping congregation who is the meaning and unity of the whole Church. He presents it to the Father, and sends it out on its mission.[25]

In sum, this 1948 report on the Anglican Communion presents an essay in self-understanding, offered both to narrate and order the rapidly evolving experience of Anglicans round the world and

25 *Ibid.*, 85-86.

to situate the conversation in older, inherited, pre-denominational forms. As an offering of the committee that prepared and presented it, the report had no official status at the time, and still has none. It provided, however, a fascinating snapshot of Anglican ecclesial discourse in the middle of the last century, which may be viewed as a last redoubt of confident consensus before the pluralizing pressures of the latter 20th century, with which we are still reckoning.

COMPARISON: CATHOLIC INTENSIFICATION

Placing the Articles of Religion and the 1948 Lambeth Conference report alongside each other (separated as they are by 400 years), a first striking difference is their description of the Holy Scriptures. In the Articles, Scripture is "God's Word," containing "all things necessary to salvation," while in the 1948 report it is "the ultimate standard of faith." In the Articles, the Holy Scriptures are the necessary touchstone for authoritative doctrinal statement, even for General Councils that are authoritatively called. Nothing may be decreed, ordained, or enforced by the Church without explication from the Scriptures. In the 1948 report, by contrast, the Scriptures are just one among a number of elements where authority is found distributed. One doubts that the Lambeth fathers thought of Scripture as an element that may need checking by other elements; the Articles, surely, would never have suggested such a thing.

We may note here, too, an interesting omission in the report. Tradition is mentioned after the Scriptures in the initial recounting of elements, but does not come up again later, leaving one to wonder whether tradition is simply subsumed under the rubric of continual interpretation of Scripture in the life of the Church. Is this all that is meant by tradition? Conversely, might *tradition* actually be subsuming the Scriptures, rather than vice versa?

A further step away from the world of *sola scriptura* by the 1948 report may be seen in its handling of councils. The Articles, for their part, pay some attention to the process by which councils are called, privileging the authority of princes, but finally emphasize that councils must cohere with Scripture. The 1948 report, by contrast, while saying nothing about how councils are convened, asserts that the authority of General Councils rests on the *consensus fidelium*, the reception of their teaching by the faithful.

If we may be tempted to chalk the foregoing contrasts up to a liberalizing modernism in the 1948 report, its primary interest in bishops will correct this idea. The Articles say very little about bishops, apart from noting in Article 36 how they are to be consecrated. Nothing is said about their authority, though Article 26 does talk about ordained ministers having Christ's "commission and authority." By contrast, the 1948 report views the bishop in a diocese as a mediator of God's authority. The authority held by the bishop is exercised in humility, as the bishop himself is under authority, presumably God's (how this might be exercised is not articulated).

Moreover, the bishop does not stand alone, but "in synodical association with his clergy and laity." As Anglican churches were organized in different parts of the world, and as the Church of England began to revive instruments of self-government apart from parliament, instruments of deliberation and decision making were forged that brought together clergy and laity with the bishops. The 1920 Lambeth Conference agreed that "it is important to the cause of re-union that every branch of the Anglican Communion should develop the constitutional government of the Church and should make a fuller use of the capacities of its members for service."[26] The report assumes that this process is well-advanced in all Anglican churches.

The report also identifies episcopacy as "the source and centre of our order." Here, "episcopacy" designates the bishops considered collectively, and the description serves not to expand the understanding of the authority mediated in the ministry of word and sacraments (just one element of the authority that is dispersed throughout the Church) but as a sort of capstone comment on all the elements. Episcopacy is linked to liturgy (which here appears for the first time) and serves as a sort of organizing principle for the whole, only emerging in a summary statement.

Since the first Lambeth Conference, the episcopacy had been called upon to supply new connective tissue for the nascent Anglican Communion. The Lambeth Conference did not create the need, which was implied in the first calls for such a gathering of bishops. Here in 1948 what was implicit in the convening of the conference was articulated in a new way. The contrast with the Articles is striking. It is not so much the contrast between a church that denies any special authority to bishops and one that affirms it. It's more the difference between the Articles' assumption that bishops have a non-weight-bearing authority relative to the royal supremacy, and the report's

---

26 *Conference of Bishops of the Anglican Communion 1920*, Resolution 14 (London: SPCK, 1920), 31; available online.

articulation of a communion of churches in which bishops are called to exercise a considerable, even unique, weightbearing role.

In articulating a role for collective episcopacy, the report was recapitulating a theme from earlier in the text: dispersed authority. The authority of the episcopate is dispersed by its nature because it involves multiple office holders. Authority in the Anglican Communion is likewise distributed among different elements that, taken together, are authoritative in the church. These elements mediate the authority of Christ and constitute a dispersed authority, set within a process that both corrects error and builds up, please God, the fullness of the Church Catholic.

The 1948 report here reflects a dynamic dating back at least to the time of St. Cyprian, who in the third century called upon the bishops of the Church collectively to bear the theological weight of unity.[27] For Cyprian, the agreement of the Church's bishops was essential. The episcopate is one harmonious multitude spread throughout the world.[28] The one Church and the one episcopate reflect the One God,[29] though the necessity for agreeing together points to a unity worked out amid underlying multiplicity.

The concurrence of the episcopate in agreeing together was in Cyprian's time an important theological datum, a sign of the Church's integrity. To be sure, the Church was diverse with respect

---

27 Robert F. Evans, *One and Holy: The Church in Latin Patristic Thought* (London: SPCK, 1972), 36-64; Benjamin Safranski, *St. Cyprian of Carthage and the College of Bishops* (Lanham, MD: Lexington Books, 2018), 1-35.

28 Cyprian, *Epistulae* 55.24.

29 *Ibid*. 43.5.

to penitential discipline, following the Decian persecution, and also diverse in baptismal discipline, as in the controversy between Cyprian and Pope Stephen. That the bishops could remain in communion with each other across such difference of practice set a powerful example.[30] As St. Cyprian wrote at the time: "The authority of the bishops forms a unity, of which each holds his part in its totality (*in solidum*). And the Church forms a unity, however far she spreads and multiplies by the progeny of her fecundity."[31]

This brings us to a final note on the 1948 report. In laying the foundation of its argument, the committee identified the need for the dispersed authority of the Anglican Communion to be willing to "defer to the common mind." The note is sounded again in the element of the *consensus fidelium*, on which councils rest. The "common mind" hearkens back to Lambeth 1930's "common counsel of the bishops in conference," on which the authority of the Communion depends. In the 1948 Report, the charitable deference exercised could be seen as a practical example of each bishop's humble submission to authority. In St. Cyprian's terms, the fact of the bishops coming to agreement is crucial for the coherence of the Communion.

---

30   *Ibid.* 55.21.

31   Cyprian, *De Lapsis* and *De Ecclesiae Catholicae Unitate*, ed and trans. Maurice Bevenot (Oxford: Oxford University Press, 1971), 5, 65.

COHERENT COMMUNION: SCRIPTURAL AND EPISCOPAL

Rereading the Articles of Religion and the 1948 report on the Anglican Communion side by side, we learn a great deal about the architecture of ecclesial authority, as the designing and assembling of dispersed pieces into a coherent, functioning whole. This is a first and fundamental lesson: that coherence itself, both theological and structural, is essential to the order of the Church, built upon charity and a shared commitment to arriving at a common mind in Christ, who is himself the foundation (1 Cor. 3:11). Properly buttressed and balanced in his apostolic Word, the Church finds her feet and her power of persuasion.

Second, Holy Scripture provides the ballast and is the primary building block of the Church as constructed by God. The Articles of Religion faithfully pass on the ancient tradition of prizing the authority of Holy Scripture, not as one element among many but as the organizing principle of authority itself. The 1948 report's affirmation of the *consensus fidelium* comes close to making this claim, but ultimately falls short. The church *receives* the Holy Scriptures. It may authorize translations, but never authorizes the Scriptures. The one who speaks for the Church will have to speak of the Holy Scriptures, as well as speak with them.

This re-valorization does not necessarily need to depend upon phrases like "ultimate standard" or "unique" to describe the authority of Scripture. To my ears this sounds overly defensive, an attempt to compensate for not-so-hidden inadequacies in the 1948 report. "The Word of God" and "all things necessary to salvation" says enough, at

least in Anglican terms. It is a formulation with medieval anteced-
ents, becomingly modest in its scope. We sometimes lose sight, in
our characteristic descriptions of Catholic and Protestant, that the
Holy Scriptures are a catholic instrument. Received by the churches,
they are also ecumenical and shared more widely than anything else
in Christianity. Just here, we may be grateful for the wise insistence
of the Articles that one portion of the Scriptures not be set against
another, since Holy Scripture in its entirety displays a coherent and
consistent witness, by divine design.

Third and finally, God's design of the Church includes, Anglicans
have said, an assurance of apostolic continuity, displayed in consistent
structural aspects. Following in the train of St. Cyprian and others,
the Church's comprehension of diversity-in-unity, spanning great distances and differences, is centered upon dioceses and bishops in a college of consensus. Here again, the 1948 report emphasizes the role of
episcopacy as a principle of coherence in the Anglican Communion.
We may rightly wonder about the unifying role of bishops today, giv-
en the apparent difficulty of sustaining common counsel. Still, the
unifying role of bishops, embodied in their commitment to conference, should not be abandoned in favor of some more bureaucratic
instrument. Longstanding pillars of Anglican ecclesiology like the
Chicago-Lambeth Quadrilateral, which have funded our ecumenical
engagement, would hardly support such a shift.

"Local adaptation" of the episcopate, however, in the words of the
Quadrilateral,[32] deserves more exploration, especially as we consider
appropriate ways of conceiving authority in the face of sustained

32   BCP 1979, 878.

disagreement, both between Anglican churches and ecumenically. The 2021 report of the Episcopal Church's Task Force on Communion across Difference, on which I served, encourages more reflection on "the exercise, role, and range of episcopal ministry, since the ministry of bishops necessarily incorporates local, regional, and worldwide aspects." This fits with the call to tend afresh to the coherence of our ecclesial structures, some of which may need to be retrofitted, reinforced, and otherwise expanded, with an eye to their evangelical and catholic coherence, set alongside the proper protection of conscience. "In a world that seeks to overcome disagreement through enforced uniformities, differentiated communion in an episcopal key may contribute a much-needed leaven of principled diversity, set within provisional structures that model humility."[33]

Looking to the next decade of life together in the Anglican Communion, let us pray that the Lord gives us the confidence and the clarity to be about this work of encouragement and common construction, "choosing with care how to build" on the foundation we have received (1 Cor. 3:10).

---

33 Task Force on Communion across Difference, *"Put Out into the Deep Water": Communion across Difference as a Christian Call*, being a Report to the 80th General Convention of the Episcopal Church, 17; available online in *The Blue Book 2021*.

Printed in Great Britain
by Amazon